Basic Alarm
Electronics

Toolbox Guides for Security Technicians

Edited by John Sanger

Basic Alarm Electronics
John Sanger

Electronic Locking Devices
John L. Schum

Upcoming Volumes

Intrusion Detection Devices: Perimeter Protection
John Sanger

Intrusion Detection Devices: Interior Protection
John Sanger

Other Guides in Preparation

Intrusion Alarm Control Equipment
Intrusion Alarm Signalling Equipment
Alarm System Power Supplies and Batteries
Peripheral Alarm System Devices
Alarm Installing Tools and Equipment
Specialized Emergency Protection Systems

Basic Alarm Electronics

JOHN SANGER

Illustrated
by Mark Russell

Butterworths

Boston   London   Singapore   Sydney   Toronto   Wellington

Library of Congress Cataloging-in-Publication Data

Sanger, John.
    Basic alarm electronics / John Sanger ; illustrated by
    Mark Russell.
        p.   cm. – (Toolbox guides for security technicians)
    Includes index.
    ISBN 0-409-90037-0
    1. Electronic alarm systems.   I. Title.   II. Series.
TH9739.S265 1988
621.389'2–dc19   87-34918

British Library Cataloguing in Publication Data

Sanger, John
    Basic alarm electronics.
    1. Electronic security equipment
    I. Title
    621.389'2

    ISBN 0-409-90037-0

Butterworth Publishers
80 Montvale Avenue
Stoneham, MA 02180

10 9 8 7 6 5 4 3 2 1

Printed in the United States of America

621.3892
SAN

Contents

About the Series

The job of protection is a serious one. Every year in the United States, more home and business owners find peace of mind through the installation of security systems. They depend on their alarm systems to function properly—their lives and property are at stake. To assist security professionals in fulfilling their obligation to customers, this series—Toolbox Guides for Security Technicians—has been created.

These volumes compile information on every aspect of alarm system planning, design, installation, service, and troubleshooting—information that will complement existing skills or become the foundation of a fledgling career. Whether you are looking for the solution to a design problem or installation snag, or seeking tips on running wire or foiling windows, this series will serve you. It is a reference library on security—the first of its kind.

Each volume is devoted to a specific topic, starting with basic alarm electronics and electronic locking devices. Subsequent works will discuss different equipment types and applications, including interior and perimeter protection devices, control panels, power supplies and batteries, signaling and monitoring systems, and outdoor protection systems. One book will be devoted to both little known and widely used tools for alarm installation and troubleshooting. Another will be dedicated to wireless intrusion detection systems. In every volume, the authors provide tips that make difficult tasks easier or simply save a few minutes of installation time.

So comprehensive is this series that the authors recognized the need for one volume to serve as a reference work for the others. This companion guide will pull together the important material contained in the other texts. Here you will find conversion tables, resistance charts, color codes, and Ohm's law, along with an installer's dictionary of security terms. Instead of thumbing through hundreds of pages searching for one piece of data, you will be able to find the information quickly in this consolidated, easy-to-use volume.

Because reliability and accuracy are essential, the contributors to this series have solid alarm industry backgrounds. Some have experience in security equipment manufacturing; many are security dealers with years of installation or service experience; others, like myself, are journalists specializing in the security field. All the contributors and writers have been selected carefully for their expertise by John Sanger, an editor with the industry's leading security publication, *Security Distributing & Marketing,* and a former alarm company owner.

Mr. Sanger, coordinator of the series and coauthor of most books, will review each work to help ensure thoroughness in content and unity in style and presentation. The material in this series has been selected with you—the security professional—in mind. The facts in these books can work for you. Read them, understand them, apply them—and watch yourself grow.

Anne Lobel Armel

Preface

You do not have to be an electronics engineer to be an alarm installer or technician. The greater your understanding of the electronic components and circuits used in security systems, however, the more efficient you will be in your profession.

Both neophytes and veterans can benefit from the material presented in this book. You may know some of it already, but there is useful information for almost everyone. This book can serve as an introductory training manual for novices and as a refresher course for those with experience. Some installers have plied their trade for years and have not taken the time or made the effort to learn simple concepts like Ohm's law. Many perform their jobs well, but they can always perform them better.

Technology is moving at a fast pace and smart professionals know they must move surely and quickly to keep up. Dry-cell-powered, relay-operated control panels are almost a thing of the past. New equipment has printed circuit boards loaded with sophisticated components such as integrated circuits. Many systems rival microcomputers in data processing abilities. Those who anticipate the future know they must learn the new technology to succeed.

And yet some, both old-timers and greenhorns, question the need for learning basic electronics theory and application. They are looking for the easy path to success. Unfortunately, there is no easy path.

Either you are committed to professionalism and the training required to achieve and maintain it, or you are not. There is no in between.

The National Burglar and Fire Alarm Association's (NBFAA) commitment to professionalism can be seen in its newly developed and highly successful National Training School. Information, similar to that contained in this book, is being presented to classrooms packed with professional alarm installers.

The starting point of the NBFAA's National Training School—and of this book—is the atom, the basic building block of matter. The atom also is the basic foundation for understanding electronics. Understanding how electrons and protons interact gives you an insight into how current flows. This material is covered in Chapter 1, where you also will learn the properties of voltage and resistance.

Chapter 2 will introduce you to the components used to build electronic equipment. You will learn the functions of various components, such as resistors and diodes. The information presented in this chapter will enable you to identify components physically and schematically. Helping you learn to read, understand, and draw simple schematic diagrams is the purpose of Chapter 3. You will use what you learned in the first two chapters to help you install, troubleshoot, and repair alarm systems.

Chapters 4 and 5 address the mathematics of electronics. You will learn what Ohm's law is, how it works, and why you need it. Other equations also will help solve tricky installation and troubleshooting problems. With the basics behind you, Chapters 6 and 7 delve into the specifics of security system circuits, components, and symbols. You will learn about various types of circuits and the numerous components that make up alarm systems. The symbols for these components will serve as your key for mapping installations.

Chapter 8 addresses power supplies. Every alarm system requires power, and selecting the proper primary and secondary power source requires more than guesswork. Learning what power supplies are, what differences in power supplies mean to a system's operation, and how power supplies operate will help you design security systems efficiently.

Wire is another necessary alarm system component. Chapter 9 guides you in wire selection and application and offers some tips for minimizing tedious wiring tasks. An assortment of tidbits about tools, tips, and techniques fills Chapter 10. One secret to success is working smarter, not harder. This chapter offers some advice on how to do just that.

The final chapter discusses safety when working with electronic equipment. Safe work habits are one mark of a professional. Good safety procedures save you time and money, and minimize damage to equipment and to your customer's property. They also may save your life. In the glossary, you will find a treasure trove of useful information that will help you identify industry jargon and technical terminology quickly.

Basic Alarm Electronics is the first in a multivolume set of books called the Toolbox Guides for Security Technicians. The intent of this volume is to provide cornerstone information. It is the foundation upon which you can build your expertise as a professional alarm installer or technician. This book has a definite place in your professional reference library. It will have a more useful place in your toolbox.

1

Basic Concepts

The language of electronics is technical, as are its concepts. It is a mathematics-oriented science. Taken at its macro level, security electronics may seem overwhelming. That is why you should begin at the micro level. Books are divided into chapters and paragraphs into sentences to help facilitate understanding. You start with small elements and build larger ones. The same is true with electronics. Look at individual concepts and components before attempting to put them in macroperspective.

An old saying is worth repeating here: It's a cinch by the inch; it's hard by the yard. Taken in small, manageable segments—inch by inch—you can accomplish most tasks. The Sears Tower began with a single cornerstone. An alarm system installation begins by mounting a single component. And understanding electronics starts with basic, simple concepts.

Power is the cornerstone of almost all electronic alarm system concepts. It is common to all systems. Tomorrow's technology may introduce totally passive systems, without power as we know it today, but those are tomorrow's systems. Today's reality is that alarm systems need active power.

The working components of power are voltage, current, and resistance. Understanding the interaction of these components helps you design, apply, install, troubleshoot, and service alarm systems. Understanding electronics theory helps you understand these components of power.

ELECTRONICS THEORY

All substances are comprised of atoms. Atoms are the building blocks of all solid, liquid, and gaseous matter. Substances that are made up of just one type of atom, such as copper, gold, oxygen, and hydrogen, are called elements. When two or more elements combine, for example, when oxygen and hydrogen combine to form water, complex compounds are created. Atoms, though the smallest particles recognizable as specific elements, also can be broken down into smaller components: electrons, protons, and neutrons.

An electron, when isolated from an atom, has a tiny electrical charge. In an atom, electrons are negatively charged particles spinning in elliptical orbits around a positively charged nucleus (see Figure 1–1). Each electron has a negative charge. Under normal circumstances, when the negative charges of the electrons that are spinning around the nucleus are added together, the total negative charge will equal the positive charge of the atom's protons. Because the two charges are equal, the net electrical charge is zero.

Neutrons, found in an atom's nucleus with protons, have no electrical charge. They are neutral, as their name implies.

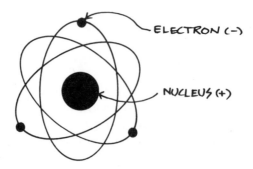

Figure 1–1. Atoms contain electrons, which have negative charges, and a nucleus, which has a positive charge.

Electrons in an atom's outermost rings, referred to as valence electrons, are bound only weakly to the nucleus. When a valence electron finds itself midway between the nuclei of two atoms, as shown in Figure 1–2, it is attracted by each nucleus. It may, at this point, leave its orbit and move into the outermost orbit on the nearby atom. It is this process of moving valence, or free, electrons from one atom to another that causes electricity to flow from one point to another.

When an electron is pulled, pushed, or otherwise freed from an atom, it drifts until it collides with another atom that will accept it. The second atom consequently throws off one of its electrons, which is accepted by another—and so forth.

Insulators and Conductors

Some substances, such as copper, contain many free electrons and give up or accept electrons readily. These substances are called conductors because they allow an electric current to pass through them easily.

Materials with very few free electrons restrict the flow of electricity and are called insulators. Air, glass, and rubber are examples of good electrical insulators.

Most electrical circuits require conductors which allow free electrons to flow, as well as a power source, an electrically operated device, or load, and a control device, such as a switch, to operate the circuit.

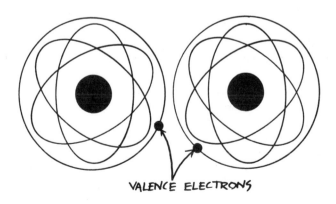

VALENCE ELECTRONS

Figure 1–2. Valence electrons may move from one atom to another.

VOLTAGE: ELECTRICAL PRESSURE

Voltage is electrical pressure. It is what forces electricity to flow. Its measurement usually is given in volts (V).

Sometimes voltage is compared to water pressure. The water that flows from your kitchen tap does not fall out; it is pushed out by a pump. Voltage works similarly. A power supply, such as a generator or battery, pushes voltage through a conductor, such as a wire.

Electrical devices, including alarm system components, must have the correct amount of voltage or electrical pressure supplied to them in order to operate properly. If too much pressure is supplied, then a device might malfunction or be damaged. If too little is supplied, the device might not work properly, if at all.

Differing Demands

Different devices have different voltage demands. Your television set requires 110 volts to operate, your flashlight only a few volts. Electronic alarm systems usually fall at the low end of the scale—operating on 24 volts or less. Typical intrusion alarm systems require 12 volts.

An entire alarm system may operate on 12 volts, but many of the components found on its control panel circuit board require considerably less power to operate. Many of these components operate on millivolts and microvolts.

A millivolt (mV) is one thousandth of a volt. If you join one thousand of them you will have one volt. A microvolt (μV) is one millionth of a volt.

You will not use millivolts and microvolts in your everyday alarm installations, but be aware of their presence in circuit board components. Twelve volts is not much power, but if you apply it to the wrong place, such as to a component that operates on 100mV, the result probably will be a puff of smoke and a damaged device.

Voltage goes by several aliases. It is sometimes called electromotive force (EMF), potential (P), or potential difference (PD). Here, the P, for potential, is not the same P as in the formula $P = E \times I$, which is discussed later.

Alternating and Direct Voltage

Two basic types of voltage exist: direct and alternating. Direct-voltage electrical pressure remains relatively constant. The pressure in alternating voltage continually changes.

A battery is an example of direct voltage. A battery rated at 12 volts maintains an electrical pressure of 12 volts, whether it is providing power to a device or sitting idle.

The voltage with which most people are familiar is the power available through plug-in outlets in homes and businesses. The voltage in these outlets changes between zero and approximately 160 volts so regularly and rapidly that an effective voltage of 110 to 115 volts is created.

Batteries and other direct voltage power supplies have terminals marked with positive (+) and negative (−) symbols, representing polarity. Power output from these terminals does not change. Positive remains positive and vice versa. That is why this type of voltage is referred to as direct voltage. It also is referred to as direct current (DC) voltage.

The electricity available through most household outlets in the United States is provided by huge generators which are housed in utility companies. Unlike direct voltage, alternating voltage, commonly called alternating current (AC), changes polarity. It switches from positive to negative to positive to negative—and so on—on a regular basis. It changes, or cycles, 60 times per second in the United States and is called 60 cycle, or Hertz (Hz), power.

Both DC and AC power have specific applications. One type of power is not superior to the other. Alarm systems use both types. Alternating voltage provides primary power for alarm systems. Most systems convert alternating to direct voltages for operational purposes. For example, 110VAC is converted to 18VAC through a transformer. The 18VAC is then converted to 12VDC to operate a control panel and peripheral devices. DC operation also allows an alarm system to have a back-up power supply. If AC power fails, a standby battery automatically takes over, providing power to the system.

Measuring Voltage

A voltmeter, as its name implies, measures voltage. When the meter's probes are connected to the positive and negative terminals on a battery, the meter reading is the battery's voltage output—the voltage available at that point, as shown in Figure 1–3.

Another useful measurement is *voltage under load* or the amount of voltage available at the component being powered. For example, if you have a 12-volt battery, a length of two-conductor wire and a light bulb, you might want to know how much voltage is available at the end of the wire. Connecting the voltmeter to the light bulb's terminals, as shown in Figure 1–4, allows you to read the voltage available to power the light. It tells you the voltage when the light is on and the battery is under a load.

CURRENT FLOW

Current is the amount of electricity flowing or the rate of flow of free electrons through a circuit. The symbol for current is I, which stands for the intensity at which electricity flows. When a large number (about 62,400,000,000,000,000,000) of electrons flow past a given point in one second, the rate of flow is one ampere (A or amp).

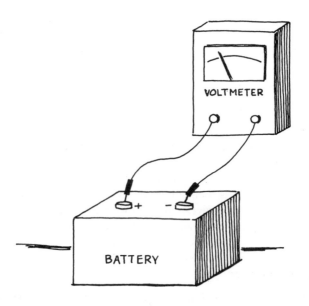

Figure 1–3. Power supply voltage can be measured by placing your voltmeter's probes directly on the supply's terminals.

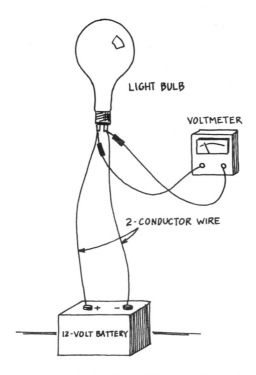

Figure 1–4.   An operating device, like a light bulb, places a load on a circuit.

Like voltage, current can be compared to water. As long as your kitchen tap is closed, water does not flow through it—if it is in good condition—yet, water pressure still exists in the pipe connecting the tap to the pumping station.

You can dramatize current flowing through a conductor with a cardboard tube and some ping pong balls. Fill the tube with balls and lay it on a table. Push one ball into one end of the tube. Another ball immediately rolls out the other end.

The ball you inserted displaced the first ball in the tube, which displaced the second ball, which displaced the third ball, and so on, until the last ball was pushed out the end. This took place almost instantaneously and each ball moved only slightly and fairly slowly, but the chain reaction was transmitted through the tube quickly.

If your tube was clear plastic, you could mark a spot on it. Then, you could watch as you tried to push 62,400,000,000,000,000,000 ping pong balls past the marked point in one second. This would represent one ampere of current flowing through a conductor.

You can have a voltage source, like a battery, without having voltage flow. A battery provides the source of voltage flow only when it is connected to a current-consuming device such as a light bulb. Current does not begin to flow until you turn on the light with a switch. Current is available, but flows only when you decide it should.

The analogy between electricity and water holds true in many instances, but we can carry the analogy only so far before it fails. There are great differences in electrons and water, and pumps and batteries. For our purposes here, the analogy works.

Direct Current

Regardless of the type of current, direct or alternating, it always flows from negative to positive. It is easiest to understand current flowing from a battery because negative and positive are identified easily by the terminal markings. Current flows from the negative terminal through a conductor to an electrical device and back to the battery's positive terminal.

This is a useful example for understanding current flow, but it is not technically correct. In reality, there is no precise starting point where current begins flowing. Think of a wheel. Which part of the wheel starts turning first? All parts turn simultaneously. The same concept applies to current flowing through a battery, a wire and an electrical device simultaneously.

Alternating Current

Current flows from negative to positive in an AC-powered system as well. Here, however, the current flow is more difficult to visualize than it was with a DC-powered system. Terminals are not marked negative and positive in an AC-powered system because they continuously change polarity.

Measuring Current

Current measurement usually is given in amperes. For many electronic alarm circuits, however, current is measured in smaller units: milliamperes and microamperes. One milliampere (mA) is one thousandth of an ampere; one microampere (μA) is one millionth of an ampere.

Breaking the circuit being tested and placing your ammeter, milli-ammeter, or microammeter in series with it allows you to measure current. The circuit is completed through the meter. If a powered device is drawing 500mA of current, your meter will read that amount regardless of where it is placed in the circuit (see Figure 1–5).

If you are measuring direct current, observe polarity. Failure to do so may damage your meter quickly and seriously.

Current Load

Any alarm system device, such as a control panel or passive infrared (PIR) detector, connected to a power source is called a load. A transformer or battery with nothing connected to it is unloaded. For simplicity, think of a load as any device that takes or draws current.

Power supplies can deliver certain levels of current. As current-consuming devices are added to the power supply, the load on the power supply is increased. If devices try to draw more power than is available, fuses may be blown, circuit breakers tripped and equipment damaged.

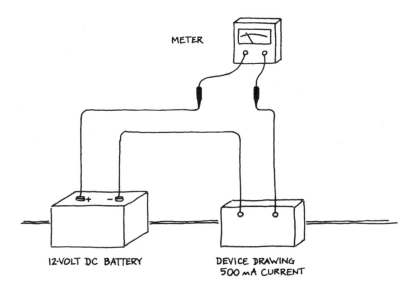

Figure 1–5. Your meter will show the same current on the positive or negative legs anywhere in the circuit.

RESISTANCE TO CURRENT FLOW

The opposition to the flow of electricity is resistance. Resistance is analogous to electrical friction. When free electrons collide with ions, an atom or group of atoms making up a metallic conductor, the free electrons give up some of their kinetic, or moving, energy to the ions in the form of heat energy.

These collisions oppose the movement of free electrons from one point to another in a conductor. They "resist" the flow.

Resistance is measured in ohms (abbreviated with the symbol for the uppercase Greek letter omega, Ω). If ohm is too small a unit to be practical, you can use kilohm (kΩ), which equals one thousand ohms, or megohm (MΩ), for one million ohms.

Metallic Conductors

Current travels from a power source through a wire (which usually is made of copper) to an electrical or electronic device. This route, a complete path through which current can flow, is called a circuit. If the circuit is continuous and remains unbroken, it is called a closed circuit.

All electronic circuits have resistance. How much resistance they have depends on the metallic components (conductors) in the circuits.

This electrical friction may cause voltage to drop and current to decrease by the time they reach the device loading the electrical circuit. How much voltage and current diminish depends on how much resistance is present. Resistance of metallic conductors depends on four factors: (1) length, (2) thickness, (3) type of metal, and (4) temperature.

Resistance of a metallic conductor is directly proportional to its length and inversely proportional to its thickness (cross-sectional area). It is dependent on the type of metal used in the conductor and, for most conductors, usually increases as temperature rises.

Measuring Resistance

Ohmmeters measure resistance and usually give readings in ohms. In addition to measuring resistance, ohmmeters provide a quick determination of whether a detection circuit, switch, or relay contact point is open or closed.

Analog-type meters, the kind with incremental scales and needles, show resistances between zero (0) and infinity (∞). The infinity symbol indicates no continuity in a circuit—that is, the circuit is open. Zero indicates a continuous, or closed, circuit.

Digital-type meters give you the same information, but display it on a digital readout rather than on a scale. These ohmmeters are more accurate than are the analog-type in determining exact resistance because a specific number is displayed. Analog meters are not as accurate, but are suitable for most installation tasks.

Regardless of the type of meter you are using, be sure to disconnect all power from the circuit being tested. Measuring resistance while power is connected will give you an erroneous reading and may damage your meter.

A specific and predictable relationship exists between voltage, current and resistance. This relationship is called Ohm's law. Chapter 4 discusses how Ohm's law applies to alarm electronics.

MEASURE OF POWER

Power typically is measured in watts (W), in honor of James Watt, the inventor of the steam engine. Power is the rate of doing work in an electric circuit. Watts indicate the amount of work being done and the amount of electricity being used. Wattage ratings are commonplace. You select light bulbs with specific ratings. Your microwave oven also is rated in watts. You may use a 75W light bulb to illuminate your front porch and a 700W microwave oven to cook dinner.

You can determine watts if you know voltage and current by using the formula $P = E \times I$ (where P is watts, E is volts and I is amps). Alarm system transformers often are rated in volt-amps (abbreviated VA). For example, a control panel may require an 18VAC, 40VA transformer. VA is a symbol meaning volts times amps. As you can see from the formula, $E \times I$ also means volts times amps. For all practical purposes in alarm work, you can think of P, W, and VA as equivalent.

2

Electronic Components and Symbols

Electronic components such as cells, batteries, and resistors are represented by specific symbols in diagrams. Think of these symbols as a type of visual electronic shorthand.

When these symbols are drawn to indicate circuits and electronic components, the resulting symbolic picture is called a *schematic diagram*. Some tips for reading schematic diagrams are included in the next chapter. In this chapter, you will find definitions and symbols for the electronic components you are likely to encounter while installing, servicing, and troubleshooting alarm systems.

WIRING CONNECTIONS

Wires are shown on schematic drawings as solid straight lines. The lines bend at 90-degree angles when turns are required.

Lines that cross in a drawing may be confusing. Do they pass each other with no electrical contact? Do they form a connection? Although variations of symbols exist, the ones shown in Figure 2–1, for wires

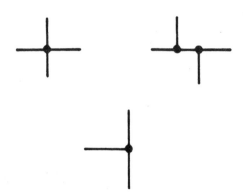

Figure 2–1.   Straight lines and dots show wiring connections.

that connect, and Figure 2–2, for wires that do not connect, are preferred because they help minimize confusion when you prepare schematic diagrams.

Unfortunately, the symbol shown in Figure 2–3 is used by some equipment designers to mean there is a connection and by some to mean there is no connection. If you encounter this symbol while reading a schematic, then check with the equipment's manufacturer or the person who drew the diagram to determine if it means the wires cross or connect.

In addition to the wire used to connect electronic parts, such as the resistors and capacitors on circuit boards, wire also is used to connect security devices (for example, detectors and bells) to other compo-

Figure 2–2.   The half circle shows no connection; one wire passes over another wire.

Figure 2–3.   When you see this symbol, check with the person who drew the diagram. It may mean there is a connection or there is not a connection.

nents. Because wire is an integral part of most electronic security systems, you will find more information about it in Chapter 9.

CELLS AND BATTERIES

A battery is made up of multiple electric cells. The symbol for an electric cell is shown in Figure 2–4.

Figure 2–5 shows the symbol for a multi-cell battery. A schematic symbol for a battery usually shows two or three cells, regardless of the number actually in the battery. It would be impractical in the small spaces of a schematic diagram to show, for example, the eight cells in a 12-volt battery or the 30 cells in a 45-volt battery.

The longer line in the symbol indicates a cell or battery's positive terminal. Some schematics show a "+" sign and some do not. The shorter line signifies the negative terminal. Likewise, a "−" sign may or may not be shown. More information on cells and batteries is included in Chapter 8.

Figure 2–4.   A single cell is represented by two sets of perpendicular lines that look like Ts. Positive (+) and negative (−) markings are not always included. The T with the narrow top signifies the negative terminal; the longer T, the positive terminal.

Figure 2–5.   Multi-cell batteries use a symbol similar to that of a single cell. This symbol can be used regardless of whether the battery has 2, 20, or 200 cells.

AC VOLTAGE SOURCES

Cells and batteries provide direct current. Alternating current also is used in alarm systems. It typically provides the primary power for a control panel.

The symbol shown in Figure 2–6 represents an AC voltage source. Because alternating current changes polarity, no polarity is indicated on the symbol.

The most readily available source of AC power is house current—110 to 120 volts. The voltage level varies somewhat, but is commonly within this range. In the United States, the AC current's frequency is 60Hz.

GROUNDS

When extra protection against dangerous voltages is needed for equipment and for the user, grounding is required. In electronics terminology "ground" may mean *earth ground* or *common ground.*

An earth ground returns potentially dangerous voltage to the earth instead of allowing it to pass into a piece of equipment or the equipment's operator. An earth ground can be effected by connecting a wire

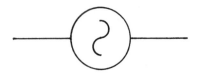

Figure 2–6.   A sine wave enclosed in a circle symbolizes an AC power source.

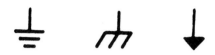

Figure 2–7. All three symbols mean ground. You may have to read the instructions for a piece of equipment to determine if the symbol is for an earth ground or a chassis ground.

from the equipment to a rod embedded in the earth. A cold water pipe also makes a good earth-ground connection if the pipe is metal and runs outside the building into the earth.

A common ground, sometimes simply referred to as *common,* is a reference point for measuring voltage in a circuit. In control panels, for example, one or two terminals may be labeled common and accept wires from several circuits.

In DC circuits, the common point is usually negative. It can be positive, however. Either positive or negative can be used as a common point for voltage measurement as long as you know the common point's polarity.

The common ground as well as the electronic circuits may be connected to the metal chassis or enclosure of a device. This makes the entire chassis or box a reference point.

The symbols shown in Figure 2–7 are those commonly used to indicate grounds. The right symbol indicates an earth ground only. The other two symbols may represent either an earth ground or a common (chassis) ground.

RESISTORS

Resistors are probably the most common electronic component and are designed to introduce a specific amount of resistance into a circuit. They are available in numerous physical sizes and electronic ratings. Figure 2–8 shows a variety of smaller resistors. A few resistors may be larger than a dime.

As a resistor works, it becomes warm. This is because it converts electrical energy into thermal energy (heat). Resistors that become too hot can become damaged, thereby changing their resistance properties.

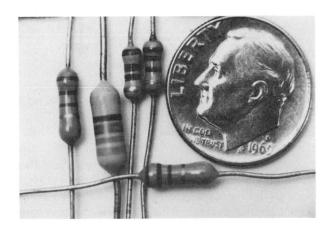

Figure 2–8. Most resistors used in alarm systems are small cylindrical devices. (Photo by author. © 1987 by John Sanger.)

Select a resistor appropriate for the job it will be doing. If in doubt, select a larger resistor than what you think will be needed. For example, a 1/2-watt resistor will work in a 1/4-watt circuit. Remember that "larger" in this sense refers to a resistor's wattage rating, not to its resistance value, which is rated in ohms.

Color Coding

A resistor is typically cylindrical and has four colored bands circling it (see Figure 2–9). These bands identify the resistor's value.

The group of bands are closer to one end of the resistor than the other end. The one closest to the end shows the resistor's first significant digit, the second band indicates the second significant digit, the third band is the multiplier and the fourth band indicates the resistor's tolerance.

Determine the bands' colors and check them against the chart shown in Table 2–1. For example, if a resistor's bands are red, green, orange, and silver, what is its value?

The red band, the first significant digit, equals 2. Green, the second significant digit, is 5. The value of the orange band is 000. Therefore, red (2), green (5), and orange (000) translate to 25,000 ohms.

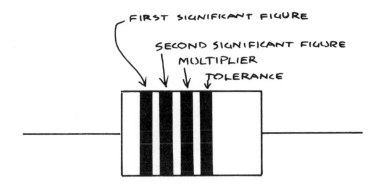

FIRST SIGNIFICANT FIGURE

SECOND SIGNIFICANT FIGURE

MULTIPLIER

TOLERANCE

Figure 2–9.   The bands on a resistor signify its value.

The silver band indicates that the resistor's tolerance is 10 percent. That is, its value may vary by 10 percent of 25,000 ohms or 2,500 ohms. The actual value of the resistor in this example might be anywhere from 22,500 ohms to 27,500 ohms.

Table 2–1.   Resistor Color Code

Color	Band 1	Band 2	Band 3	Band 4
Black	0	0		
Brown	1	1	0	
Red	2	2	00	
Orange	3	3	000	
Yellow	4	4	0000	
Green	5	5	00000	
Blue	6	6	000000	
Violet	7	7	0000000	
Gray	8	8	00000000	
White	9	9		
Gold			× 0.1	+/− 5%
Silver			× 0.01	+/− 10%
No Band				+/− 20%

Figure 2–10.   In a schematic drawing, a sawtooth shape symbolizes a resistor.

Fixed Resistors

Resistors with values that do not change are called *fixed resistors.* The symbol for a fixed resistor is shown in Figure 2–10.

Although a resistor may have a 10 percent tolerance, its actual value remains relatively constant unless it becomes damaged. All resistors exhibit some resistance changes in response to temperature fluctuations, but these changes are usually insignificant.

Common types of fixed resistors are *composition* and *metal film* resistors. Composition resistors consist of a thin coating of carbon on a ceramic tube. Because carbon is a poor conductor of electricity, these resistors, though small, can create large resistance.

Metal film resistors use a thin metallic film instead of carbon and can be manufactured to more precise values. They also are less sensitive to temperature fluctuations than their carbon counterparts.

Variable Resistors

Sometimes it may be necessary to change the resistance in a circuit; in these cases, *variable resistors,* often called *rheostats* or *potentiometers,* are used. (Potentiometers usually are referred to as "pots.")

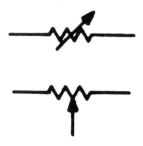

Figure 2–11.   The arrow through the symbol for a resistor represents a variable resistor.

For most practical purposes, the terms rheostat and potentiometer are interchangeable. Rheostats usually are used on heavy-duty AC circuits, while potentiometers are used on low-power circuits.

One difference between the two devices is the number of terminals on the devices. Potentiometers usually have three terminals; rheostats usually have two. Figure 2–11 shows the schematic symbols for two- and three-terminal variable resistors.

Combining Resistors

Resistors may be combined to increase or decrease resistance. You may need a 1,000-ohm resistor and find your parts bin empty, for example. If you have two 500-ohm resistors, you can connect them in series for a total resistance of 1,000 ohms: resistances in series are additive. Therefore, 1,000 ohms of resistance can be created in a variety of ways if a single 1,000-ohm resistor is not available.

The formula for calculating resistance in series is:

$$R_T = R_1 + R_2 \ldots + R_n$$

where R_T is the total resistance. The letter n signifies the total number of resistors in the series.

If resistors are connected in *parallel*, then current will flow through both paths. If both resistors are equal, equal current will flow through both. If they are not equal, then more current will flow through the path with less resistance.

The formula for determining the resistance for two resistors connected in parallel is:

$$R_T = \frac{(R_1 \times R_2)}{(R_1 + R_2)}.$$

And the formula for calculating the resistance of several resistors connected in parallel is:

$$R_T = \frac{1}{(1 / R_1) + (1 / R_2) \ldots + (1 / R_n)}$$

where R_T is the total resistance.

CAPACITORS

Voltage is stored in *capacitors*. The insulating material, the *dialectric*, in a capacitor helps determine the capacitance of a device of a given size. Capacitors generally are classified by the type of dialectric they contain. The common schematic symbol for a capacitor is shown in Figure 2–12 and it is used regardless of the type of capacitor.

The basic unit of capacitance is the farad. In most circuits, the farad is too large to be practical. Microfarad, which is equal to one millionth of a farad, usually is used. The notation μF signifies microfarad. A picofarad, or one trillionth of a microfarad, is a still smaller unit. The symbol pF denotes picofarad.

Most capacitors are rated at two voltage levels: breakdown and working voltage. The breakdown voltage is the maximum voltage the dialectric can withstand without breaking down.

Working voltage is the maximum DC voltage that can be placed across the capacitor's plates safely. Exceeding the working voltage may damage or destroy the capacitor and nearby components.

Ceramic Capacitors

A capacitor with a wafer of ceramic material between two silver plates is called a *ceramic capacitor*. Most look like discs, although some are rectangular. They are electrically the same regardless of their shapes. Working voltages for most ceramic capacitors range from about 50 to 1,600 volts.

Mica Capacitors

Thin strips of mica sandwiched between interconnected plates make up a *mica capacitor*. Common values range from 5 pF to 0.01 μF and their working voltages from 200 to 50,000 volts.

Figure 2–12. This symbol is used for non-polarized capacitors.

Paper Capacitors

If a higher capacitance is necessary than a mica or ceramic capacitor can provide, *paper capacitors* can be used. These capacitors are made by placing strips of waxed paper between two long strips of tin foil. Capacitance ranges from about 0.0001 μF to 1 μF and working voltages from 200 to 5,000 volts.

Synthetic Film Capacitors

Synthetic film can be used in lieu of paper. Such capacitors usually are named for the types of films used. *Mylar, polyester* and *polystyrene* are types of synthetic film capacitors.

Film capacitors can operate over a wider range of temperatures than can paper capacitors. They also are more precise, due to their smaller tolerances. The capacitance range for film capacitors is usually from 0.001 μF to 2 μF with working voltages ranging from 50 to 1,000 volts.

Electrolytic Capacitors

The previously discussed capacitors are *nonpolarized*. They can be placed in a circuit without regard to polarity. *Polarized* capacitors are designed to work only in DC circuits and polarity must be observed. The schematic symbol for a polarized capacitor looks like the symbol for a regular capacitor—with the addition of a "+" sign, as shown in Figure 2–13.

The most common polarized capacitor is the *electrolytic capacitor*. If you took one apart, you would find a pasty substance between aluminum foil plates. Because of its composition, an electrolytic capacitor's values range from about 0.47 μF to 10,000 μF. Some have higher values. Working voltage ranges from as little as 3 to more than 700 volts.

Figure 2–13. Adding a positive (+) sign to the capacitor symbol indicates that the capacitor is polarized.

Figure 2–14.   An arrow through the symbol for a capacitor means it is a variable capacitor.

Tantalum Capacitors

Like electrolytic capacitors, *Tantalum capacitors* only can be used in DC circuits. These capacitors tend to be smaller than their electrolytic counterparts. They are more precise and are not as prone to drying out when not in use.

Tantalum capacitors are usually more expensive than electrolytic capacitors. They have much smaller capacitances, usually ranging from 0.5 μF to 50 μF, and their working voltages rarely exceed 50 volts.

VARIABLE CAPACITORS

Most capacitors have fixed values, as do most resistors. Also, similar to resistors, some are available with variable values. The schematic symbol for a *variable capacitor* is shown in Figure 2–14.

DIODES

A device that allows current to flow in one direction only is called a *diode*. The common schematic symbol for a diode is shown in Figure 2–15.

Semiconductor diodes will break down at certain voltage levels. The specifications for a diode will list its peak inverse voltage (PIV) or peak reverse voltage (PRV)—the point at which it will break down.

Figure 2–15.   Diodes allow current to flow in only one direction.

Figure 2–16. The zener diode symbol indicates that the diode functions differently from regular diodes.

Zener Diodes

A *zener diode*, schematically depicted in Figure 2–16, is a specialized version of a semiconductor diode. It responds to reverse voltage differently than do other diodes. The voltage rating of a zener diode is the point at which it begins to conduct when reverse biased. This point often is called the "avalanche point."

Light-Emitting Diodes

Like other diodes, *light-emitting diodes*, or *LEDs*, conduct in one direction only. As its name implies, the device emits light—it glows when forward biased.

Red, green and yellow (amber) are common colors for LEDs. Other colors, including blue and purple, are available, and some emit light in the infrared region. The common symbols for LEDs, regardless of the color of light emitted, are shown in Figure 2–17.

LEDs are durable devices intended for low-voltage circuits. Most operate on 3 to 6VDC. A sure way to burn one out is to apply 12VDC to it. Remember to use a resistor to limit voltage if you are using a 12VDC power source.

Because LEDs are forward biased and light only when polarity is observed, they can be used as polarity checkers. Dual LEDs, two LEDs

Figure 2–17. The two arrows by the symbol for a diode indicate that it is a light-emitting diode (LED).

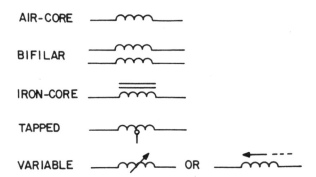

Figure 2–18.   Different symbols represent different types of coils.

in one package, also are available. A dual LED will glow one color when voltage is applied. Reversing polarity will cause the other color to glow.

You can apply AC voltage to some LEDs and, if the AC frequency is low enough, you can see them blink on and off as the AC cycles. At higher frequencies, they still blink on and off, but they do so much too fast for the human eye to see separate blinks.

COILS

Winding wire around a core produces an electronic component called an inductor, commonly known as a *coil*. The core may be iron, a cardboard tube or any of several materials. In alarm equipment, for example, you can find coils in relays and transformers. Figure 2–18 shows the schematic symbols for the types of coils you are most likely to encounter.

TRANSFORMERS

If you wind two or more coils around a single core, you will create a *transformer*. Symbols for common transformers are shown in Figure 2–19.

When the number of turns in a transformer's primary winding are the same as in its secondary winding, the device simply isolates the

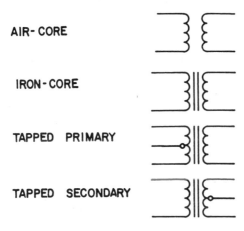

AIR- CORE

IRON - CORE

TAPPED   PRIMARY

TAPPED   SECONDARY

Figure 2–19. Symbols for transformers indicate the type of core and whether it has a tapped primary or secondary coil.

load from the power source. A *step-down transformer* is created when there are fewer turns in the secondary than in the primary winding.

Step-down transformers commonly are used to provide power to control panels and other devices in alarm systems. For example, an 18VAC step-down transformer may be required to convert 110VAC to a voltage level required by a control panel.

If a transformer's secondary winding is greater than its primary winding, a *step-up transformer* is created. These types of transformers rarely are used in alarm system applications.

SWITCHES

A *switch* is a device that makes (connects) and/or breaks (disconnects) an electrical connection. It selectively allows current to pass.

Single-Pole Switches

Switches that make contact in only one position, such as common light switches, are called *single-pole, single-throw* (*SPST*) switches. The schematic symbol for this type of switch is shown in Figure 2–20. As

Figure 2–20.   A single-pole, single-throw (SPST) switch is an on-off type of switch.

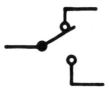

Figure 2–21.   A single-pole, double-throw (SPDT) switch allows you to control two circuits.

you can see from the diagram, only two positions are possible. It is basically an on-off switch.

Adding an extra connection to a single-pole switch lets it make contact with either of two separate points, as shown in Figure 2–21. Because this switch has a single pole and two potential contact points, it is called a *single-pole, double-throw (SPDT)* switch.

Double-Pole Switches

Combining two SPST switches in a single package produces a *double-pole, single-throw (DPST)* switch, as shown in Figure 2–22. A DPST switch lets you control two electrically separate circuits with one lever

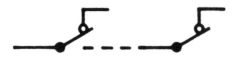

Figure 2–22.   A double-pole, single-throw (DPST) switch opens or closes two circuits simultaneously.

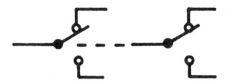

Figure 2–23. A double-pole, double-throw (DPDT) switch simultaneously opens two circuits and closes two circuits.

or button. The two "throws" operate in unison—either they are both on or they are both off.

Double-pole, double-throw (DPDT) switches, as shown in Figure 2–23, allow you to achieve two separate SPDT actions with the throw of a single switch. A DPDT switch can be used in lieu of any of the other three switch types simply by connecting circuits to the appropriate terminals.

Multi-Position Switches

Occasionally, more connections are needed than can be provided by DPDT switches. Slide switches may have up to two poles and four positions each (DP4T). If you need more poles and/or positions, you will need a *rotary switch*. Schematic symbols for rotary switches vary depending on the number of poles and positions, but they look similar to the one shown in Figure 2–24.

Two varieties of rotary switches help you do the precise job you want to do. One type, the make-before-break switch, maintains the

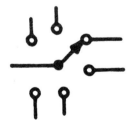

Figure 2–24. A rotary switch allows you to control numerous circuits.

Figure 2–25.   A spring-loaded momentary-contact switch makes or breaks a circuit only while the switch's lever or button is thrown or pushed.

first connection until the second connection is made. The other type, the break-before-make switch, does just the opposite.

Momentary-Contact Switches

If you need to make or break a circuit connection briefly, then return the circuit to its original condition, a *momentary-contact switch* can be used. This type of switch allows you to operate it without having to move the lever or button of a latching switch from one position to another.

Normally open spring-loaded, momentary-contact switches often are used as panic buttons in alarm systems. Normally closed versions also are available for other applications. The schematic symbol for a NC momentary-contact switch is shown in Figure 2–25.

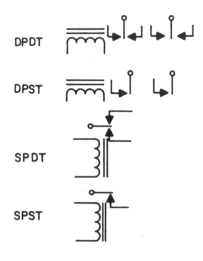

Figure 2–26.   Relays are automatic switches.

Figure 2–27. A fuse may be considered to be a type of switch because it opens a circuit when too much current is present.

Figure 2–28. Circuit breakers act like fuses, but they can be reset manually.

RELAYS

Automatic switching can be achieved by using *relays*. Most relays consist of two parts, a coil and a switch. When voltage is applied to a relay's coil, a switch is engaged and/or disengaged—either making or breaking an electrical connection. Relays can be found with the four basic switch types (SPST, SPDT, DPST, DPDT). Figure 2–26 shows schematic symbols for these relay types.

FUSES AND CIRCUIT BREAKERS

A switching device used to protect sensitive electronic circuits is a *fuse*, which is a thin piece of wire encased in a glass tube. When current reaches a specific level, the wire melts, disconnecting or switching off the circuit. The schematic symbol for a fuse is shown in Figure 2–27.

Circuit breakers are similar to fuses because they break circuits when current exceeds predetermined levels. Unlike fuses, they do not have to be replaced. They can be reset and used again. Figure 2–28 shows the schematic symbol for a circuit breaker.

3

Schematics, Other Diagrams, and More Symbols

A schematic diagram presents a road map of an electronic circuit. It helps you navigate various turns and observe and avoid roadblocks. It is a diagram of a scheme—in this case, an electronic scheme.

Schematics are a lot like road maps that show how towns and cities are interconnected. A four-lane highway looks different than a secondary road on a road map. Likewise, different kinds of lines mean different things on schematic drawings.

SYMBOLOGY

Schematic drawings use symbols, such as the ones shown in Chapter 2, instead of pictorial drawings. If electronic components were drawn the way they look in reality, schematics would be much larger, more cumbersome, and more difficult to read.

The language you speak is symbology. Words without reference keys mean nothing. For example, if you heard the word "klarn" you would not know what it means. You would have no reference point. (Klarn is not a real word. I made it up.)

Some of you will recognize the word "sesquipedalian." Some of you will not. It is a real word. Whether or not it symbolizes anything to you depends on a reference point or definition. (Sesquipedalian is an adjective meaning characterized by the use of long words.)

"Stop" is a word almost everyone recognizes. Your parents probably said this word to you many times when you were a child. Therefore, you have a history of reference points for this word.

Schematic symbology is similar to these word-related examples. Once you have reference points for symbols, you will understand their meanings. Symbology is written communication. You cannot speak a symbol in the same way you can a word. But symbols, alone and in groups, let us convey complex thoughts simply and easily.

SIMPLE CIRCUITS

Symbols for common electronic components are included in the previous chapter. You will be introduced to a few more symbols in this chapter to help you understand how schematic drawings are read and drawn.

Flashlight Circuit

A simple electronic circuit is contained in a flashlight. The components, excluding the flashlight's case, include two batteries, conductors (wires), a switch, and a light bulb. A pictorial representation of this circuit is shown in Figure 3–1.

Each of these electronic components has a schematic symbol. The symbols are shown in Figure 3–2.

If you replace the pictorial representations of the components with their symbols, you will get a *schematic* representation of the circuit. Figure 3–3 shows a schematic diagram of the flashlight's electronic circuit.

Power Supply Circuit

Another example of a simple circuit is shown in Figure 3–4. The only symbol of a power supply in this diagram which was not included in Chapter 2 is the symbol for the plug.

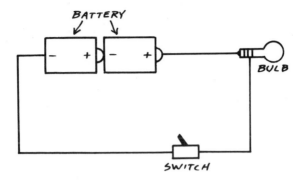

Figure 3–1. This drawing shows a flashlight's electronic circuit.

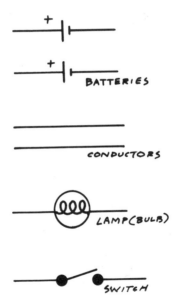

Figure 3–2. These unconnected symbols show the components in a flashlight's circuit, but give no clue to the device's operation.

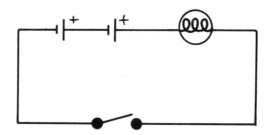

Figure 3–3. By connecting the symbols, a schematic diagram of a flashlight's electronic circuit may be made.

If you read the diagram from the left, you notice there is a male plug and a fuse connected to a transformer's primary winding. A diode is connected in series with the secondary winding and an electrolytic capacitor is connected in parallel across the transformer's output. A fixed resistor also is connected in parallel across the output. Because DC power is polarized, the power supply's outputs are marked with a "+" and "−" sign.

You cannot tell how much voltage is available at the + and − terminals from this diagram. The output voltage depends on the value of the components used.

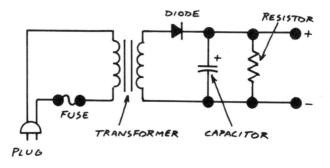

Figure 3–4. A power supply may be drawn schematically to show the kinds of components needed in the electronic circuit.

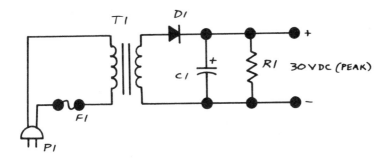

CI - 100 MICROFARAD ELECTROLYTIC - 50 VDC
DI - 50 PIV 1 AMPERE
FI - ½ AMP. 125 VOLTS
PI - MALE LINE PLUG
RI - 10,000 Ω 1 WATT CARBON
TI - 115 V PRIMARY - 12V SECONDARY - 1 AMPERE

Figure 3–5. Alphanumeric designators may be added to schematic drawings.

The diagram shown in Figure 3–5 is similar to the one in Figure 3–4, except that alphanumeric designators have been added. These designators direct the user to a key which shows the values of the various components.

ALPHANUMERIC DESIGNATORS

Designators make schematics more useful. In Figure 3–4, it is possible to determine the types of components needed to build a power supply. Figure 3–5 shows the exact components needed to build a power supply that will provide a peak output of about 30VDC.

The letters used to identify the components are fairly standard. Not all people use them, but they are the norm for most. Common designators are shown in Table 3–1.

Numerals are added to letters to indicate the number of this type of component being used. For example, T1 indicates the first trans-

Table 3–1.   Alphanumeric
Designators[a]

Designator	Component
ANT	antenna
B	battery
C	capacitor
CB	circuit board
CR	zener diode
D	diode
F	fuse
I	lamp
IC	integrated circuit
K	relay
L	inductor, choke
LED	light-emitting diode
M	meter
P	plug
Q	transistor
R	resistor
RFC	radio-frequency choke
RY	relay
S	switch
SPK	speaker
SR	selenium rectifier
T	transformer
TP	test point
U	integrated circuit
VR	voltage regulator
Y	crystal

[a] Sometimes more than one designator is used
to identify a type of component.

former. If a second transformer were used, it would be labeled T2. The numbers help you identify components in the components list.

Although the use of standard designators is encouraged, it is not mandatory. As long as a components list is keyed to a schematic's markings, you will be able to determine the correct components.

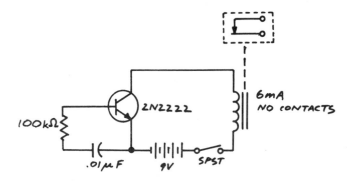

Figure 3–6.   Some schematics show component values and part numbers.

Alternate Designation Method

Instead of including alphanumeric designators on a diagram, you can write in the value designation (for example, 9V or 9VDC, for the battery) or component number (for example, 2N2222, for the transistor) next to each symbol, as shown in Figure 3–6.

Transistors frequently are used in electronic equipment. Symbols for common transistors are shown in Figure 3–7.

Schematic Exercises

As an exercise to check your understanding of schematics, look at the circuit shown in Figure 3–8. Can you identify the resistors, capacitors, LEDs, transistors, and battery?

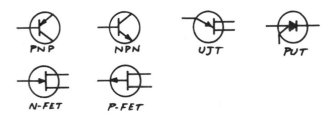

Figure 3–7.   Different types of transistors are represented by different schematic symbols.

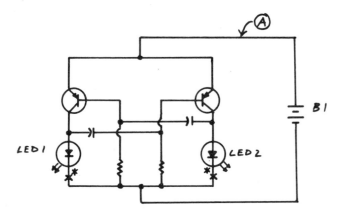

Figure 3–8. Connecting the components as shown here creates a circuit that will alternately flash two LEDs.

Alphanumeric designators identify the components and you can check them against the parts list. Value designations also are given on the diagram.

If you would like to put this circuit together, you can find the parts at most electronics stores. The parts list is shown in Table 3–2. Once you have connected all the components, you will have a device with two LEDs that alternately blink on and off.

House the components in an attractive box. Paste your business card on the front and drill small holes (the same size as the LEDs you are using) on each side of the card. Insert and glue the LEDs into the holes so they stick out past your card. You now have a small atten-

Table 3–2.   Parts List for LED Flasher

Item	Description
B1	3VDC Battery
C1, C2	Capacitors, 47pF
LED1, LED2	LEDs, visible (any part numbers)
Q1, Q2	Transistors, pnp, 2N3906 (or similar)
R1, R2	Resistors, 100K-ohm

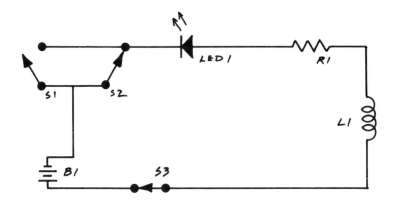

Figure 3–9.   A simple-to-build circuit tester helps you track down defective alarm sensors.

tion-getting device to take with you to the next home show at which your company exhibits.

There is one component missing from the diagram: a switch that will turn the blinking LEDs on and off. This switch should be installed along the conductor on the positive side of the battery near the point marked "A."

Another device you can build is shown in Figure 3–9. It is a latching circuit tester that will help you track down detectors triggering inadvertent alarms. The parts list is shown in Table 3–3.

Table 3–3.   Parts List for Circuit Tester

Item	Description
B1	12VDC battery
LED1	2.2V, 50mA LED
L1	5V, DPDT relay
R1	68-ohm, 10%, 1/2-watt resistor
S1	NO switch from initiating device
S2	NO switch from relay
S3	NC external reset switch

TROUBLESHOOTING WITH SCHEMATICS

Understanding what components do, as well as where they are located in circuits, helps you find and correct problems. For example, a schematic might show a 1,000-ohm resistor between two components. If you measure resistance and find it very high, it may indicate the resistor is defective.

If a flashlight is not working, a schematic will help you start your troubleshooting procedures. (In actual practice, you probably would not refer to a schematic for a device as simple as a flashlight. Following the diagram in Figure 3–3 helps present the concept of troubleshooting with schematics, however.)

Looking at the flashlight's schematic, you might decide to measure the voltage across the series-connected batteries. Your voltmeter should read 1.5 volts if its leads are placed across the positive and negative terminals of one battery.

If one battery reads 1.5 volts and the other 0 volts, then one battery is bad. If both are tested and have 0 volts, then both are bad. If you get a 3-volt reading, the batteries are good and the problem lies elsewhere in the circuit.

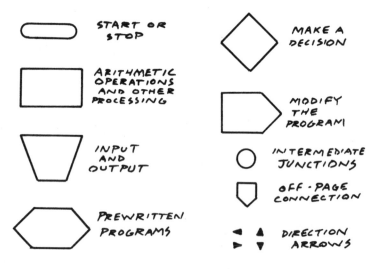

Figure 3–10.   Standard flowchart symbols help to promote uniformity.

In this simple circuit, there are only three other components: the lamp, the switch, and the conductor (wire). Deductive reasoning tells you if the batteries are good, one of the other components is bad.

Because current must flow through the bulb for the flashlight to operate, you might test for a good bulb. Place the negative probe of your meter on the battery's negative terminal and the positive probe on the bulb's lead farthest from the battery. If you get a voltage reading, the bulb is good. If no voltage reading is obtained, the bulb is bad.

Test the switch in a similar manner. Place your voltmeter's negative probe on the battery's negative terminal. Place your meter's positive probe on the positive side of the switch. After closing the switch's contacts, you should get a voltage reading if the switch is good.

If you have not discovered the problem after testing the batteries, bulb, and switch, the problem must be in one of the conductors. There is a broken or loose wire somewhere in the circuit.

FLOWCHARTS

Although flowcharts are not diagrams of electronic circuits, they can be useful in diagraming tasks. For example, you can use them to establish testing and troubleshooting procedures.

Like schematic diagrams, flowcharts have special symbols. The most common ones are shown in Figure 3–10.

Figure 3–11 shows an example of a troubleshooting procedure to help find a problem in the circuit of the flashlight previously mentioned. The flowchart takes you through the troubleshooting procedures step by step.

PROGRAM EVALUATION AND REVIEW TECHNIQUE

The Program Evaluation and Review Technique (PERT) was developed by the United States Navy for the Polaris program. It is a tool for planning, executing and controlling complex tasks.

PERT's main objective is to furnish information. The technique does not make decisions. It generates information so you can make decisions.

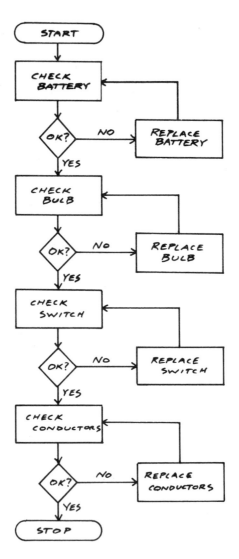

Figure 3–11. A flowchart for troubleshooting a flashlight's electronic circuit might look like this.

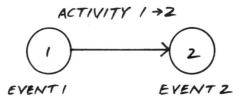

Figure 3–12. Symbols depict events and activities in PERT charts.

Using PERT

The first step in using PERT is setting a goal. The next step is identifying the activities required to achieve the goal. For example, if your goal is to sharpen your pencil, then several activities are required. You must pick up the pencil, walk to the pencil sharpener, insert the pencil, turn the handle, remove the pencil, and return to your desk. That is a simplistic example, but it gives you an idea of the PERT process.

Figure 3–12 shows one segment of a PERT chart. Circles represent events. The arrow between two events represents an activity. Events are physical or intellectual accomplishments and do not consume time or resources. Activities represent the work or expenditure of resources to move a project from one event to the next.

PERT charts can be used for planning and controlling alarm system installations. In a very simple example, assume you are installing one

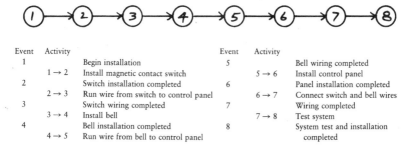

Event	Activity		Event	Activity	
1		Begin installation	5		Bell wiring completed
	1 → 2	Install magnetic contact switch		5 → 6	Install control panel
2		Switch installation completed	6		Panel installation completed
	2 → 3	Run wire from switch to control panel		6 → 7	Connect switch and bell wires
3		Switch wiring completed	7		Wiring completed
	3 → 4	Install bell		7 → 8	Test system
4		Bell installation completed	8		System test and installation completed
	4 → 5	Run wire from bell to control panel			

Figure 3–13. A PERT chart for an alarm installation with one installer might contain eight events.

46 BASIC ALARM ELECTRONICS

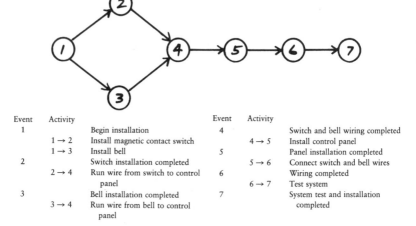

Event	Activity		Event	Activity	
1		Begin installation	4		Switch and bell wiring completed
	1 → 2	Install magnetic contact switch		4 → 5	Install control panel
	1 → 3	Install bell	5		Panel installation completed
2		Switch installation completed		5 → 6	Connect switch and bell wires
	2 → 4	Run wire from switch to control panel	6		Wiring completed
3		Bell installation completed		6 → 7	Test system
	3 → 4	Run wire from bell to control panel	7		System test and installation completed

Figure 3–14. A PERT chart's branches indicate two installers are working at the same time.

magnetic contact switch, one control panel, and one bell. The PERT chart for the installation might look like the one in Figure 3–13 if one installer was working. If two installers were working, the chart might look like the one in Figure 3–14.

All events and activities necessary to accomplish your goal must be included for PERT to be effective. Once you have made a list of these events and activities, you can construct a PERT network in a logical sequence. Adding time estimates makes the network a useful scheduling tool.

If you want more information about PERT, visit your local library. Many college-level business management textbooks contain detailed descriptions of the technique and its myriad uses.

ELECTRONICS SHORTHAND

Component symbols are not the only ones you will encounter as an alarm installer. The language of security electronics is rife with other symbols and abbreviations.

Much of the language is coded in shorthand. You will encounter numerous symbols, abbreviations, and acronyms in equipment catalogs, brochures, specification sheets, and instruction manuals.

ABBREVIATIONS AND ACRONYMS

Table 3–4 shows common electronics and alarm industry abbreviations and acronyms. Definitions for many of them can be found in the glossary. Commonly used electronic signs and symbols are included in Table 3-5.

Many electronics terms, values, and measurements have prefixes. Megohm is an example. The prefix, mega, when added to ohm gives you a new reference value. In this case, mega is shortened to meg because ohm begins with a vowel. Meg or mega, which means million, changes ohm to million ohms. Ergo, if you saw a notation like "1.1 megohm-resistor," then you would know the resistor's value was 1.1 million ohms. Table 3–6 shows you common prefixes used in electronics.

Because electronics is a mathematics-based science, mathematics symbols are commonplace. These shorthand notations, like the ones shown in Table 3–7, tell you which operations to perform to determine values based on mathematical operations and what relationships exist between values.

Table 3–4. Abbreviations and Acronyms

A	ampere (amp)
AC	alternating current
Ah or AH	ampere hour
Amp	ampere
ASCII	American Standard Code for Information Interchange
AWG	American wire gauge
CATV	cable television
CCTV	closed-circuit television
dB	decibel
DC	direct current
DIP	dual-inline package
DPDT	double-pole, double-throw
DPST	double-pole, single-throw
EOL or E-O-L	end-of-line
EMI	electromagnetic interference
EPROM	erasable programmable read only memory
GHz	gigahertz

Table 3–4. (*continued*)

Hz	Hertz
IC	integrated circuit
IR	infrared
k	kilo
kHz	kilohertz
Kilo	thousand
LED	light-emitting diode
mA	milliampere
Meg or Mega	million
MHz	megahertz
Micro	one millionth
Milli	one thousandth
Mux.	multiplex
NC	normally closed
NEC	National Electrical Code
NFPA	National Fire Protection Association
NO	normally open
PC	printed circuit
PCB	printed circuit board
PIR	passive infrared
PROM	programmable read only memory
RAM	random access memory
RF	radio frequency
RFI	radio frequency interference
ROM	read only memory
SPDT	single-pole, double-throw
SPST	single-pole, single-throw
Telco	telephone company
UHF	ultra high frequency
UL or U.L.	Underwriters Laboratories
V	volt(s)
VOM	volt-ohm-milliameter
VHF	very high frequency
X	trans
Xfmr	transformer
Xmtr	transmitter
μ (Greek *mu*)	micro
μA	microampere
Ω (Greek *omega*)	ohm(s)

Table 3–5.   Electronics Signs and Symbols

C	capacitance
cps	cycles per second (Hz)
D	distance
E	voltage (Ohm's law)
G	conductance
I	current (Ohm's law)
L	inductance
n	multiplication factor
P	power
P_i	input power
P_o	output power
R	resistance (Ohm's law)
T	time
V	velocity
Z	impedance
°C	degrees Celsius
°F	degrees Fahrenheit
π (Pi)	3.14159 . . . (usually rounded to 3.14 or 3.1416)
Δ	change of

Table 3–6.   Metric Prefixes

Prefix	Symbol	Value
Tetra	T	1,000,000,000,000
Giga	G	1,000,000,000
Mega	M	1,000,000
Kilo	k	1,000
Hecto	h	100
Deca	da	10
Deci	d	0.1
Centi	c	0.01
Milli	m	0.001
Micro	μ	0.000001
Nano	n	0.000000001
Pico	p	0.000000000001

Table 3–7.   Common Mathematical Signs and Symbols

Symbol	Meaning
·	logic multiplication symbol
∞	infinity
+	addition symbol, plus, positive
−	subtraction symbol, minus, negative
±	plus or minus, positive or negative
×	multiplication symbol
÷	division symbol
/	division, expressive of a ratio
=	equal symbol
≐	approximately equal to
≈	approximately equal to
≠	not equal to
~	similar to
<	less than
≮	not less than
>	greater than
≯	not greater than
→	approaches
:	is to, proportional to
∴	therefore
#	number
%	percent
@	at, at the rate of
π	Pi, approximately 3.14159
()	parentheses, encloses common group of terms
[]	brackets, encloses common group of terms which also includes terms enclosed in parentheses
{}	braces, encloses common group of terms which also includes terms enclosed in brackets
°	degrees (temperature or arc)
′	minutes, prime
″	seconds, double prime
. . .	(elipsis) and beyond

4

Ohm's Law

Here is a quiz question: Is there a relationship between current and voltage? The answer is no—and yes.

If, on the one hand, you mean does high voltage always have high current and low voltage always have low current, then the answer is no. For example, your car's battery is 12VDC but it may be required to deliver several hundred amperes to start your car. The digital clock-radio on your nightstand operates on 120VAC and probably consumes less than one ampere.

On the other hand, if you mean is there an arithmetic relationship between current and voltage, the answer is yes. The relationship between current, voltage, and resistance is called Ohm's law.

Generally, if you increase voltage, current flowing to a load also increases, and vice versa. A car's battery is a good analogy. If the battery is weak and below its 12-volt nominal rating, your car may not start because the battery cannot provide enough current to the starter motor.

Another relationship in Ohm's law exists between current and resistance. When one increases, the other decreases.

Because current is inversely proportional to resistance, we can write Ohm's law as:

$$I = E/R$$

In this equation, I represents current (in amperes), E represents voltage (in volts), and R represents resistance (in ohms).

Think of I and R as two children on a seesaw. When I goes up, R comes down, as shown in Figure 4–1. That is what is meant by inversely proportional.

What this means to you is simple: you can control current flow by changing resistance. Increasing resistance decreases current flow. Decreasing resistance increases current flow.

You probably increase and decrease resistance and current flow more often than you realize. When you turn up the volume on a radio or adjust the dimmer switch on a light, you are participating in practical uses of Ohm's law.

As you have seen from this one equation, you can control current by increasing or decreasing voltage or resistance. To help you remember and use the equation, look at the drawing in Figure 4–2. If you cover I with your finger, you have E over R. That represents the basic equation of I = E/R.

Ohm's law is probably the most important equation alarm installers will use. Voltage, current, and resistance are present in every alarm system and electronic circuit. In addition, it is a simple formula to use. For example, if you want to double the amount of current flowing, you can double voltage or cut resistance in half.

Learning and applying Ohm's law is not a training course exercise. It has practical applications. Ignoring it can cost you money. Knowing

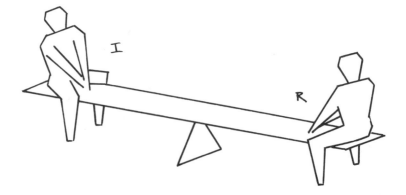

Figure 4–1. Resistance (R) and current (I) are inversely proportional. When one goes up, the other goes down.

Figure 4–2. You can remember the variations of Ohm's Law (I = E/R) with this diagram. Cover the letter for the element you want to calculate, then perform the calculation as indicated by the remaining two letters. For example, to calculate current, cover I. Then divide voltage (E) by resistance (R). To determine voltage, cover E. Then multiply current (I) by resistance (R). To determine resistance, cover R. Then divide voltage (E) by current (I).

it can save you money. The amount of current flowing determines, for example, the size of wire you will need for a bell circuit. The larger the wire, the greater its cost. You will know what size wire you need if you use Ohm's law and will not have to guess.

VARIATIONS OF THE LAW

If you recall your high school algebra, you remember that equations can be written different ways. Therefore, the basic equation, I = E/R, also can be written as:

$$R = E/I.$$

Resistance can be determined if you know or can measure voltage and current.

You can use a multi-meter to measure a circuit's resistance. Ohm's law gives you an idea of what the resistance should be before you measure it.

For example, if you measure a battery's voltage at 12 volts and a meter in the circuit tells you 500mA of current is present, then the circuit's resistance will be E/I (E divided by I) or 12/0.5. (Remember to change milliamps to amps for the calculation.) Ergo, R = 24 ohms.

Ohm's law also can be written as:

$$E = I \times R.$$

Table 4–1.   Conversion Factors

To convert	To	Do this
milliamperes	amperes	divide milliamperes by 1,000
microamperes	amperes	divide microamperes by 1,000,000
millivolts	volts	divide millivolts by 1,000
microvolts	volts	divide microvolts by 1,000,000
kilohms	ohms	multiply kilohms by 1,000
megohms	ohms	multiply megohms by 1,000,000

Convert measurement units to standard units when using Ohm's law.

This variation of the law is useful because you can calculate the amount of voltage in a circuit if you know or can measure current flow and resistance.

Remembering Standards

Whenever using Ohm's law, remember to use volts, amperes, and ohms. Table 4–1 shows how to convert commonly used measurements to the standard measurements required by Ohm's law. Table 4–2 shows the values of the multiples of common measurements used in security electronics.

Table 4–2.   Value Multiples

Unit	Ohm's Law Symbol	Multiple	Value
ampere	I	milliampere (mA)	1/1,000 ampere
ampere	I	microampere (μA)	1/1,000,000 ampere
volt	E	millivolt (mV)	1/1,000 volt
volt	E	microvolt (μV)	1/1,000,000 volt
ohm	R	kilohm (kΩ)	1,000 ohms
ohm	R	megohm (mΩ)	1,000,000 ohms

Milli and micro are common prefixes for amperes and volts. Kilo and mega (or meg) are common for ohms.

5

Other Electronic Formulas

A scientific law is a general, verifiable statement describing the behavior of entities or the relationships between phenomena or concepts. In addition to Ohm's law, other laws, rules, formulas, and effects are useful to people who work with electronics. These principles of electronics set forth specific characteristics of magnetism, voltage, current, and resistance. You can find more information on these and other electronics laws in numerous books at your local library.

Ampere's Law: Current flowing in a wire generates a magnetic flux which encircles the wire in the clockwise direction when the current is moving away from the observer.

Coulomb's Law: The force (F) of attraction or repulsion between two charges (Q) of electricity at two points in an isotropic medium is proportional to the product of their charges (or to the magnetic pole strengths) and is inversely proportional to the square of the distance (d) between them:

$$F = (Q_1 \times Q_2) / d^2$$

Unlike charges attract each other and like charges repel each other. (Coulomb's law also is called the Law of Charges, Law of Electric

Charges, Law of Electrostatic Attraction and the Law of Electrostatic Repulsion.)

Distributive Law: The arithmetic (algebraic) law that states that $x(y + z)$ is the equivalent of $xy + xz$.

Faraday's Law: The voltage induced in a conductor moving in a magnetic field is proportional to the rate at which the conductor cuts magnetic lines of force.

Faraday's Laws of Electrolysis: (1) In electrolysis, the mass of a substance liberated from solution is proportional to the strength and duration of the current. (2) For different substances liberated by the same current in a certain time, the masses are proportional to the electrochemical equivalents of the substances.

Joule Effect: The heat occurring from current flowing through a resistance.

Joule's Law: The rate at which heat is produced by current flowing in a constant-resistance circuit is proportional to the square of the current.

Kirchoff's Current Law: At a junction of three or more branches in an electric circuit, the total current entering the junction must equal the total current leaving the junction.

Kirchoff's Voltage Law: The algebraic sum of the voltages in a closed path in an electric circuit is equal to zero.

Laplace's Law: The strength of the magnetic field at any given point due to any element of a current-carrying conductor is directly proportional to the strength of the current and the projected length of the element, and is inversely proportional to the square of the distance of the element from the point in question.

Law of Averages: In probability and statistics, the law stating that for a large sampling of events, the numerical probability value will be more closely approached than when the sampling is small.

Law of Charges: (See Coulomb's law.)

Law of Electric Charges: (See Coulomb's law.)

Law of Electromagnetic Induction: (See Lenz's law.)

Law of Electrostatic Attraction: (See Coulomb's law.)

Law of Electrostatic Repulsion: (See Coulomb's law.)

Law of Induction: (See Faraday's law.)

Law of Large Numbers: In probability and statistics, the law stating that with a large sample, the sample average is extremely likely to approximate the population average. Often erroneously called the Law of Averages.

Law of Magnetism: Unlike magnetic poles attract and like magnetic poles repel each other. (See also Coulomb's law.)

Lenz's Law: The current induced in a circuit due to a change in the magnetic flux through it or to its motion in a magnetic field is so directed as to oppose the change in flux or to exert a mechanical force opposing the motion. If a constant current flows in a primary circuit (A) and if by motion of A or the secondary circuit (B), a current is induced in B, the direction of the induced current will be such that, by its electromagnetic action on A, it tends to oppose the relative motion of the circuits. In other words, a magnetic field created by an induced current is always in the direction that opposes any change in the existing field.

Maxwell's Rule: Every part of an electric circuit is acted upon by a force tending to move it in the direction that results in the maximum magnetic flux being enclosed.

Pythagorean Theorem: A theorem of plane geometry which states that for a right triangle, with sides of lengths a, b, and c, where c is the side opposite the right angle, it is always true that $a^2 + b^2 = c^2$.

Reflection Law: The angle of incidence is equal to the angle of reflection.

Speed of Light: The velocity of light is approximately 180,000 miles per second.

Speed of Sound: The speed of sound is approximately 1,129 feet per second in air and 4,800 feet per second in water.

FORMULAS AND CONVERSIONS

As useful as scientific laws are, sometimes high school level mathematics, algebra, and geometry help alarm installers do their jobs. For example, if distance is given in meters, you may want to change it to yards or feet. If an electronic device's operating temperature is given in degrees Celsius, you may want to convert the temperature to Fahrenheit.

If a glass-breakage detector's specifications say it will work on windows up to 32 square feet, you need to know how to calculate a window's area. If an audio discriminator will detect sounds effectively in a room of up to a certain volumetric size, you need to know how to calculate volume. Here are some formulas to help you:

Helpful Formulas

- Circumference of a circle: multiply diameter by 3.1416
- Area of a circle: multiply square of diameter by 0.7854
- Diameter of a circle: multiply circumference by 0.31831
- Area of a triangle: multiply base by 1/2 perpendicular height
- Area of a square or rectangle: multiply length by width
- Area of a parallelogram: multiply length by width (where width is a perpendicular line connecting the two long sides)
- Area of a pentagon (five equal sides): square length of one side and multiply by 1.72
- Volume of a cube: multiply length by width by height
- Volume of a sphere: cube diameter and multiply by 0.5236
- Surface area of a sphere: square diameter and multiply by 3.1416
- Volume of a cylinder: multiply the square of the radius of the base by 3.1416 and multiply by the height

Conversion Factors

You occasionally may need to convert one unit of measurement to another. Here's how:

- Inches to centimeters: multiply inches by 2.54
- Inches to millimeters: multiply inches by 25.4
- Feet to centimeters: multiply feet by 30.48
- Yards to meters: multiply yards by 0.914
- Miles to kilometers: multiply miles by 1.61
- Millimeters to inches: multiply millimeters by 0.03937
- Centimeters to inches: multiply centimeters by 0.3937
- Meters to feet: multiply meters by 3.2808
- Meters to yards: multiply meters by 1.0936
- Kilometers to miles: multiply kilometers by 0.621
- Ohms/kilometer to ohms/1,000 feet: multiply ohms/kilometer by 0.3048
- Ohms/1,000 feet to ohms/kilometer: multiply ohms/1,000 feet by 3.281
- Fahrenheit to Celsius: subtract 32 from degrees of Fahrenheit and multiply by 5, then divide by 9
- Celsius to Fahrenheit: multiply Celsius degrees by nine, divide by 5, then add 32

6

Security Circuits

Security circuits, like other electronic circuits, exist in two basic configurations: series and parallel. A variation is a combination series-parallel circuit, which incorporates both types into a single circuit. All three types of detection circuits can be present in today's intrusion alarm systems.

Series circuits often are called *closed* circuits because they form a continuous unbroken path along which current can flow. In the alarm industry, they typically are referred to as normally closed (NC) circuits or loops because they are closed when in the "ready" mode. An example of a series circuit is shown in Figure 6–1.

Most intrusion circuits use detection devices with normally closed relays or switches connected in series with each other. When the system's control panel detects a momentary loss of continuity in a normally closed detection circuit, it triggers an alarm if the alarm system is armed. If the system is not armed, most control panels indicate that the system is not ready because continuity in the series loop does not exist.

Parallel circuits also are used in intrusion alarm systems. These *open* circuits most often are used for hold-up and panic buttons and similar devices, but some open-circuit intrusion detection devices are available. A normally open (NO) circuit, shown in Figure 6–2, oper-

59

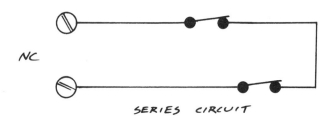

Figure 6–1. A series circuit forms a complete path, allowing current to flow.

ates the opposite of a normally closed circuit. Closing or shorting a normally open circuit triggers an alarm.

Confusion about terminology for devices connected to normally closed and normally open circuits has existed for some time. For example, a magnetic contact switch designed for a series (normally closed) circuit would be considered a normally closed device when the magnet is next to the switch. It would be normally open when the magnet is away from the switch.

Likewise, relays can be either normally closed or normally open, depending on whether they are energized or not. Some manufacturers and installers label them based on their energized state; others, based on their de-energized state. Make sure the device you plan to use will function in the circuit you intend to install it in before you install it.

Throughout this book, and the other books in this series, *normally closed* refers to series circuits and the devices that are closed when in the ready mode and open to trigger an alarm. *Normally open* refers to parallel circuits and the devices that are open when in the ready mode and close to trigger an alarm.

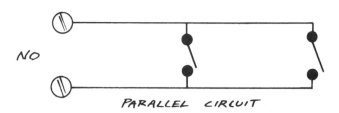

Figure 6–2. A parallel circuit does not allow current to flow until a short occurs.

CIRCUIT VARIETIES

Currently, several varieties of normally closed, normally open, and combination intrusion detection circuits can be found in use in alarm system installations. Some offer circuit supervision. That is, if a fault in a component or the wiring occurs, it is annunciated locally and/or remotely. Degrees of supervision exist, ranging from minimal to complete.

Some detection circuits, typically normally open circuits, are not supervised. If a wire is broken, for example, there is no indication of the fault at the control panel and some detection devices may be rendered ineffective.

Simple Normally Closed Loop

The two-wire, unsupervised, closed-circuit loop, which looks like the series circuit shown in Figure 6–1, is sometimes called a "hot loop" because it has a single positive and negative connection. It is common in older alarm systems but it is being replaced by two-wire supervised loops in newer ones.

The hot loop begins at the control panel's terminals and ends at the last normally closed device on the circuit. A single wire could be run for this type of circuit. A twisted pair of wires usually is used for convenience, however.

Troubleshooting wiring problems can be time-consuming in this type of circuit. Finding a broken wire, for example, may require checking the circuit at numerous points on a hit-and-miss basis.

A short between the two wires in the circuit also can be troublesome. First, when a short occurs, there is no indication at the control panel that a problem exists. Second, all detection devices beyond the short will be shunted, that is, they will be removed from the circuit. Third, like finding a broken wire, locating a short also becomes a hit-and-miss procedure.

Four-Wire Loop

The four-wire or double circuit loop, shown in Figure 6–3, provides true negative and positive voltage to the circuit. A short between the negative and positive legs would either trigger an alarm or cause the control panel to show a fault condition.

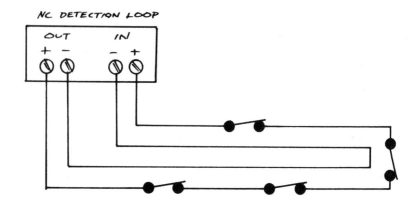

Figure 6–3. A four-wire loop provides circuit supervision to detect breaks and shorts.

Placing a jumper across the negative terminals in the control panel converts the four-wire loop to a simple normally closed loop (see Figure 6–4). Doing so removes the supervisory feature of the four-wire circuit.

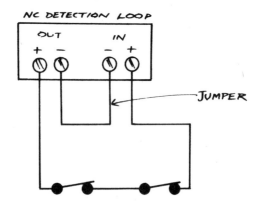

Figure 6–4. A four-wire loop can be made into a hot loop at the expense of circuit supervision.

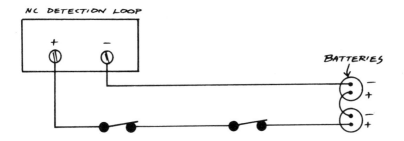

Figure 6–5. The end-of-line battery loop also provides circuit supervision.

End-of-Line Battery Loop

The end-of-line (EOL) battery loop is similar to the hot loop, except that the end-of-line battery loop provides power at the end of the circuit, as shown in Figure 6–5. For convenience, the batteries may be placed inside the control panel or in a nearby protective enclosure.

End-of-Line Resistor Loop

Most currently available control panels offer two-wire supervised detection circuits. Supervision is achieved by adding a resistor at the end of the loop. A normally closed end-of-line (EOL) resistor loop is shown in Figure 6–6. Many EOL-supervised circuits accept normally closed and normally open detection devices as shown in Figure 6–7.

The EOL resistor allows the control panel to differentiate between a short and an opening in the detection circuit. If the circuit is opened, by a broken wire, for example, the control panel would "see" no

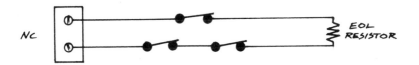

Figure 6–6. Changes in resistance, above or below specific tolerances, on an end-of-line resistor loop trigger an alarm, or signal a fault in the circuit.

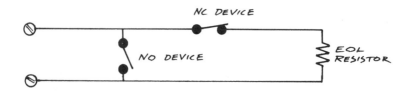

Figure 6–7. Some end-of-line resistor loops accept normally closed and normally open detection devices.

resistance. Likewise, if a short occurred, the control panel would detect a different resistance from that set up by the EOL resistor.

Auxiliary Security Loops

Open-circuit loops, requiring normally open devices connected in parallel, often are found in control panels as 24-hour auxiliary circuits. Frequently, they are used as panic and hold-up alarm circuits. These circuits are always on and trigger an instant alarm, regardless of whether the alarm system is armed or disarmed.

SHUNTING CIRCUITS

Sometimes special needs arise when one or more detection devices need to be shunted, or bypassed, in a detection loop. Often all that is needed to shunt devices is a simple single-pole, single-throw switch. Closed- and open-circuit configurations can be shunted, as shown in Figure 6–8.

TROUBLESHOOTING DETECTION CIRCUITS

Successful and efficient troubleshooting depends on logical reasoning, organization, and sometimes, luck. The more logical reasoning and organization you have, the less luck you will need.

Logical reasoning is little more than understanding the circuits you are troubleshooting. If you know what kind they are, you will know how they are supposed to function. Then, by comparing how they actually are functioning, to how they should be functioning, you will have the basic information necessary to begin your troubleshooting.

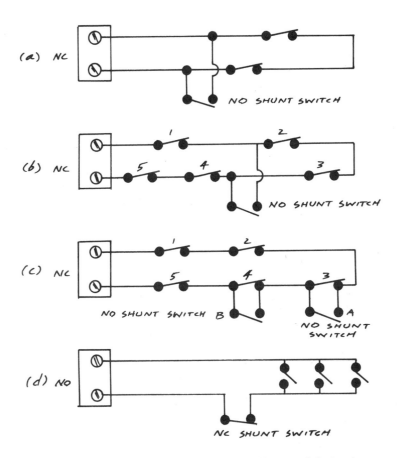

Figure 6–8. (a) Closing the NO shunt switch will bypass all devices between it and the end of the circuit. (b) Closing the NO shunt switch removes devices 2 and 3 from the circuit, while leaving the other devices in the circuit. (c) Closing shunt switch A removes device 3 from the circuit and closing shunt switch B removes device 4 from the circuit, without affecting the other devices. (d) Opening the NC shunt switch removes from the circuit all devices between the switch and the end of the circuit.

Troubleshooting proceeds much more quickly if you are organized. Develop a plan that suits you and the type of systems you install. This plan should set forth specific steps to help you track down problems. For example, you might begin by checking all detection circuits' resistances at the control panel, then proceeding to check the detection devices on each circuit.

Your plan may include the path you will take, such as tracing the first circuit from beginning to end. Or, it may specify the types of detection devices, such as foil tape on windows, you will check first.

Unfortunately, there is no magic troubleshooting formula into which you can insert information and end up with an answer. The only formula that comes close is this one: knowledge + logical reasoning + planning + persistence = success. In lieu of a magic formula, here are some tips to help you with your troubleshooting tasks.

Basic Troubleshooting Procedures

The type of detection circuit will determine, to some extent, the troubleshooting procedures you will employ. Some general techniques apply to almost all circuit troubleshooting, however.

One such technique is the divide-and-conquer procedure. Using the specific troubleshooting techniques for the type of loop you are using, find the middle of the detection circuit. From that point, determine if the problem lies toward the control panel or the end of the circuit.

Then, find the mid-point of the faulty half of the circuit. Test the circuit again and determine in which direction the problem exists. Continue dividing the faulty portion of the circuit until you have isolated the problem to a small section of the circuit, then to a single segment of wire or detection device.

Simple Normally Closed Loop

Because you cannot check voltage on a simple normally closed circuit, or hot loop, you will have to disconnect the circuit from the control panel's terminals, as shown in Figure 6–9. Set your volt-ohm-milliameter (VOM) or multi-meter to check continuity, usually on its Rx1 or a similar setting. Then place the meter's leads on the disconnected circuit wires.

If the circuit is good, the meter's needle will swing over and indicate a continuous circuit. If the circuit is bad (that is, open or broken), the meter will show no continuity.

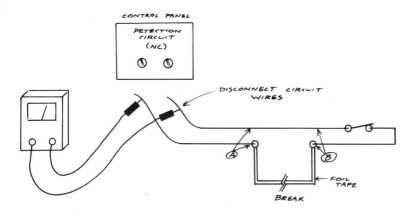

Figure 6–9. Remove wires from control panel before checking continuity on a normally closed, unsupervised ("hot") loop.

Find the middle of the circuit at point A in the diagram, and check the circuit again. If the meter shows an open circuit, the problem is between the test point and the control panel. If the meter shows continuity, the problem lies further down the loop.

In the example, checking at point A would reveal an open loop between the test point and the end of the loop. Checking at point B reveals a continuous loop from that point on, indicating the the trouble lies between points A and B.

A short on a hot loop, where the circuit's two legs touch, as shown in Figure 6–10, is more difficult to locate than a break in the detection circuit. After disconnecting the circuit from the control panel's terminals, begin checking the loop starting with the first detection device and proceeding toward the end of the detection circuit.

Place your meter's leads on the far side of each detection device, as shown in the diagram. If your meter shows no continuity, the short is farther down the loop. When your meter shows a short, the trouble lies between that point and the point previously checked.

Four-Wire Loop

After setting your VOM or multi-meter to its low-voltage DC scale, read the voltage on the loop output and input terminals. The amount of voltage present on the output terminals will depend on the kind of

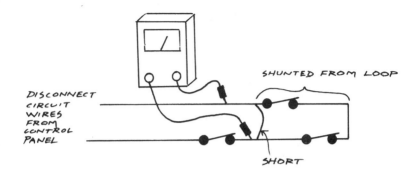

Figure 6–10.   Locating a short on a hot loop sometimes requires beginning your troubleshooting with the first detection device on the loop and working your way to the end of the loop.

control panel you are using. Check the installation instructions and specifications if you are not sure how much voltage should be present.

If the correct voltage is present on both sets of terminals, then the circuit is complete and is not the source of trouble. If there is no voltage on the output terminals, a problem may exist with the control panel.

If there is no voltage on the input terminals, the detection loop is lacking continuity. That is, there is no complete path for voltage to flow from the output terminals back to the input terminals, indicating a problem such as a broken or disconnected wire, broken foil tape or a defective device.

Before you start a tedious search for the problem, check to be sure all doors and windows with detection devices attached to them are closed. You may, for example, find a door that was not closed securely. Closing it might solve the problem. If all doors and windows are closed, and there is still no voltage present on the detection circuit's input terminals in the control panel, the problem lies somewhere in the circuit.

Begin your search by finding the approximate mid-point of the detection circuit and measure voltage again see Figure 6–11). If voltage is present at "A," the problem lies between the mid-point and the end of the circuit. If no voltage is present, the problem is toward the control panel.

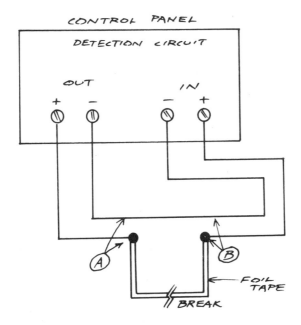

Figure 6–11. Troubleshoot a four-wire loop by measuring voltage along the circuit.

Continue tracing the voltage until you lose it. If, as shown in the figure, you had checked at "B," you would have found no voltage. Deductive reasoning would tell you the problem lies between points A and B, and in this example is a window with broken foil tape.

A short between the positive and negative legs on a four-wire loop returns power to the output terminals instead of letting it continue through the circuit to the input terminals.

Following a voltage-tracing procedure similar to the one used to locate a break in the circuit, check the circuit. Continue dividing the circuit in half and measuring voltage. When your meter shows no voltage, or a significant loss in voltage, you are close to the problem.

End-of-Line Battery Loop

You can use troubleshooting procedures similar to those used for four-wire loops for end-of-line battery loops. Remember that power is coming from the end of the loop, not from the control panel, so you will have to adjust your testing procedures accordingly.

End-of-Line Resistor Loop

A problem on an EOL resistor loop can be tracked down in a similar manner to finding one on a simple normally closed loop. Use the divide-and-conquer technique, measuring resistance along the circuit. Remember the EOL resistor adds a specific resistance to the circuit. When you find the section of the loop that shows either no resistance or very high resistance, you are close to the problem.

Tips and Techniques

Sometimes there is no substitute for experience. The education you get from experience will be invaluable to you if you remember the lessons you have learned. Lessons learned by others also can be invaluable if they are shared.

Figure 6–12.   Pins and sockets on plug-in connectors can oxidize or corrode, and resistance can build up. (Photo by author. © 1986 by John Sanger.)

The following potpourri of tips and techniques may be useful to you in your circuit-troubleshooting efforts.

- Finding cracks, especially small, hairline cracks, in foil is difficult. Foil is metal. It contracts and expands with cold and heat. Try chilling it by spraying circuit chiller or heating it with a portable hair dryer with your meter attached to the foil's take-off connectors. The cold or heat may cause the cracked foil to separate enough to show up on the meter. Warning: do not spray the circuit chiller on a hot window or blow hot air on a cold window—you may break the glass.
- Inspect plug-in connectors, like the one shown in Figure 6–12. Oxidation and corrosion on the pins and sockets can cause resistance to build up in circuits.
- Foil tape with nicks and scratches, as shown in Figure 6–13, eventually will cause problems. Repair or replace damaged foil as soon as it is discovered.

Figure 6–13.   Although still providing a good circuit because it is still intact, scratched or nicked foil tape may cause problems later. (Photo by author. © 1984 by John Sanger.)

- Good solder joints help prevent trouble from developing in electrical connections (see Chapter 9 for soldering tips).
- Double-check DIP switch settings. Use a small screwdriver, as shown in Figure 6–14, to press the tiny slide or rocker switches to help ensure that they are properly seated and making good contact.

Swingers

A *swinger* is a momentary opening of a closed circuit or a momentary closing of an open circuit. The short duration of the open or closed condition makes them annoying and extremely difficult to locate.

In a zoned system, you know the swinger-causing detection device is limited to one of the devices on a particular zone. Once you have narrowed down the number of intrusion sensors that might be causing the problem, you have a choice: either attach specially designed swinger-detection devices to each sensor or physically test each sensor. If you opt for the latter procedure, here are some suggestions:

Figure 6–14. DIP switches that are not seated properly may not be making good electrical connections. (Photo by author. © 1986 by John Sanger.)

1. Measure and record the resistance of the entire loop and of each sensor. High resistance may indicate a potential problem.
2. Attach your meter's leads to the terminals of each sensor and tap the sensor while watching your meter's needle. If the needle moves as you tap the sensor, you may have found the problem sensor. (Remember: some meters are dampened and may not "spot" the opening or closing of a device's relay or reed switch if it is very fast.)
3. With your meter attached, gently pull on the wire connection—as you might pull on door cords—and watch for erratic needle movement.
4. Visually inspect each sensor and tighten connections.
5. Check foil tape for hairline cracks or cuts.
6. Check tamper switches on devices where corrosion might occur, such as outdoor siren and bell boxes. Corrosion causes resistance to build up.

If your meter is not sensitive enough to detect swingers, disconnect the system's bell, siren, and/or digital communicator. Attach a small buzzer to the terminals that provide voltage when the system goes into alarm. Arm the system and repeat your testing procedures.

When the buzzer sounds, you have located the problem. Do not stop there, however. Continue testing the circuit. You may find multiple problems.

Other Problems

If the system continues to trigger inadvertently and randomly, other problems may exist. Circuit wiring, sensors, and/or the control panel may be picking up radio-frequency interference (RFI).

Most RFI problems can be solved by making sure the control panel is properly grounded. If the circuit wiring is acting as an antenna, you may have to install shielded wire.

Electronic devices are subject to failure. If you have checked the detection circuit thoroughly and found no problems, then you will have to turn to the system's individual devices to solve the problem. This may require replacing contact switches, motion detectors, and possibly, the control panel.

7

Security Components
and Symbols

Like electronic components, security devices and components also have special symbols. They're used on blueprints and floor plans to show the type and location of each alarm system component.

Figure 7–1 shows how you might start drawing a floor plan using security symbols. The diagram shows the approximate locations of two recess-mounted magnetic contact switches and three passive infrared sensors. To finish the drawing you'd need to add the other components—a control panel, digital keypad and siren/speaker—needed to complete the system.

Intrusion alarm system symbols usually are squares, diamonds, triangles and circles. Whenever possible squares and diamonds should be 5/32-inch on each side. Triangles should have a 3/16-inch base and circles should have a 5/32-inch diameter.

LETTER DESIGNATORS

Letter designators are placed inside or to the right of the geometric symbols and give the symbols meaning. For example, a Z inside a square signifies a zoned control panel. A Z and an 8 would indicate an

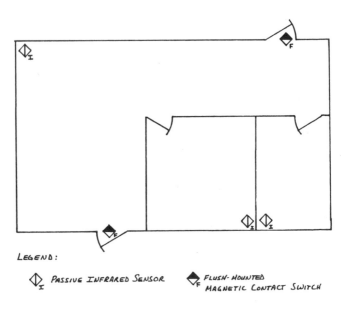

LEGEND:

◈ PASSIVE INFRARED SENSOR   ◆ FLUSH-MOUNTED
                               MAGNETIC CONTACT SWITCH

Figure 7–1. Security symbols allow you to show the type and location of each system component in floor plans and blueprints.

eight-zone control panel. Table 7–1 shows some common letter designators. Underwriters Laboratories (UL) classification letters are placed to the left of symbols, if the equipment is UL-listed and is installed in a system requiring a UL certificate. For example, AA to the left of the

Table 7–1. Common Letter Designators

A	police/fire connect
B	direct (central station) connect
C	digital communicator
D	digital keypad
DX	derived channel equipment
E	emergency power supply/ battery
F	flush
G	glass break detector
H	capacitance/proximity sensor
I	passive infrared

Table 7–1. (*continued*)

IF	infrasonic
J	multiplex
K	keyswitch
L	tape dialer
LC	line-cut monitor, telephone
M	microwave
O	outdoor/weatherproof
P	photoelectric
Q	listen-in
R	remote
RT	long-range radio transmitter
S	sound detector/discriminator
SP	splice point/junction box
T	toggle/pushbutton
U	ultrasonic
V	vibration/shock
W	wireless
X	transformer
Y	supervised wireless
Z	zone

symbol for a control panel indicates a UL Grade AA direct (central station) connect device.

Figure 7–2 shows the standard symbols for intrusion alarm system components.

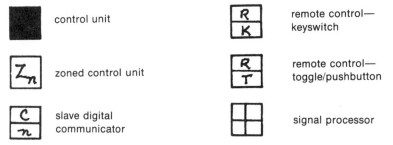

control unit

remote control— keyswitch

zoned control unit

remote control— toggle/pushbutton

slave digital communicator

signal processor

Figure 7–2. Standard symbols combined with letter designators allow you to illustrate succinctly an almost limitless number of security devices. A lower case *n* represents *number*. For example, Z_n in the symbol for zoned control unit indicates the number of zones. Replace the *n* with the correct number for the control panel you are using.

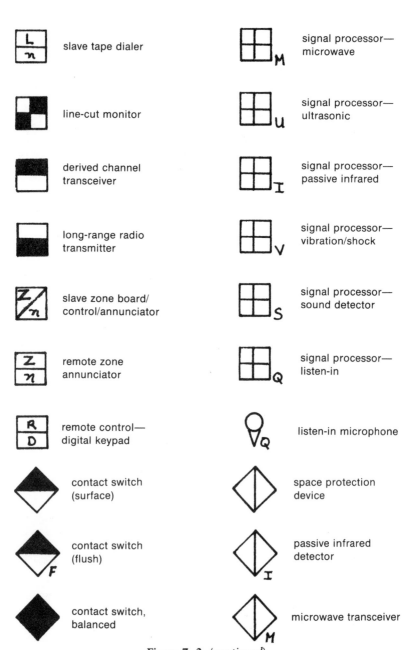

Figure 7–2. (*continued*)

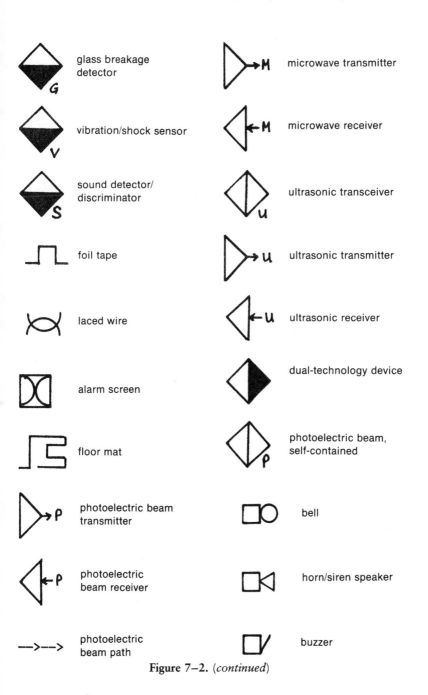

glass breakage detector

microwave transmitter

vibration/shock sensor

microwave receiver

sound detector/discriminator

ultrasonic transceiver

foil tape

ultrasonic transmitter

laced wire

ultrasonic receiver

alarm screen

dual-technology device

floor mat

photoelectric beam, self-contained

photoelectric beam transmitter

bell

photoelectric beam receiver

horn/siren speaker

photoelectric beam path

buzzer

Figure 7–2. (*continued*)

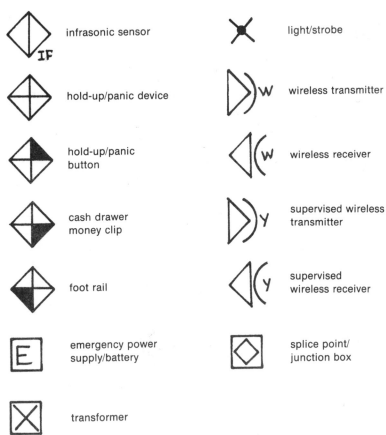

infrasonic sensor	light/strobe
hold-up/panic device	wireless transmitter
hold-up/panic button	wireless receiver
cash drawer money clip	supervised wireless transmitter
foot rail	supervised wireless receiver
emergency power supply/battery	splice point/ junction box
transformer	

Figure 7–2. (*continued*)

8

Introduction to Power Supplies

Although power supply can mean a transformer, a battery or a rectifier-filter (with or without a charging circuit) that converts AC to DC power, alarm installers usually apply the term to the three components as a group. Most standby power supplies used in alarm systems use rechargeable batteries (Figure 8–1).

A power supply starts at its step-down transformer, which converts 117VAC to a lower voltage—usually 12 to 18VAC for most intrusion alarm systems. From the transformer, power is provided through a two-conductor cable to an electronic device containing a rectifier and filter circuit, where the AC power is converted to DC power. A charging circuit often is contained within a power supply; in this way, the supply's rechargeable battery is being charged constantly, as long as primary (AC) power is present.

The critical factor in selecting a power supply is determining the load it must support. Hence, your first step will be to determine how much power will be required by all power-consuming devices connected to the supply. You then must calculate how long you want to supply standby power in case primary power fails.

Figure 8–1. Rechargeable batteries are common in today's alarm systems.

The power supply you choose should be voltage regulated: it must be able to hold a fixed voltage output over a range of loads and charging currents.

LOST POWER

Blinking digital clocks remind us that there has been a power outage. If power failed for the clock, it also failed for all other electrical and electronic devices—including alarm systems. Unlike most digital clocks and other appliances, most alarm systems switch over to back-up power. The switch-over occurs even though the outage may last only seconds.

Accidents and storms can disrupt power in large areas for many hours. Four to eight hours of reserve power will operate alarm systems through most power failures. In case AC power fails, however, the batteries you install should be capable of powering alarm systems for extended time periods.

Longer outages do occur. Some may last for 24 hours or longer. If a power failure occurs after a business closes on Friday, the alarm system should have adequate standby power to be operating when the business owner comes to work Monday morning.

Time Requirements

As a rule of thumb, intrusion alarm systems providing moderate levels of security should be able to operate for at least 48 hours on reserve power. For higher security, 96 hours is the minimum.

Both cases pertain to systems in normal, non-alarm conditions. Enough power should be available at the end of the standby time to power the systems through three complete alarm cycles. If the system you are installing requires a UL certificate, be sure to check UL's requirements for standby power.

Cycles and Voltage

In the United States, 60-cycle power is usually standard and reliable. But while the cycles may be constant, supplied voltages may vary. What you assume to be a 117VAC power may range from 100 to 130VAC.

Older homes and businesses sometimes have voltages as low as 90VAC. This may be caused by corrosion on the wires and terminals connecting the utility transformer to the premises' wiring. Low voltages can damage microprocessor-based equipment as easily as high voltages.

Microprocessor components, especially integrated circuits, are designed to operate at specific voltages. They are not very tolerant of voltage fluctuations. Low voltages may cause components to try to pull additional power, further lowering their tolerance. High voltages can burn them out.

Measure voltage at the power source, and measure again at the voltage input terminals on the equipment you are powering. If the voltage at either point is beyond the equipment's operating limits, ask the manufacturer for suggestions. If the voltage is above 125VAC or below 105VAC, report it to the electric utility serving your area.

SUPPLYING POWER

Before connecting peripheral components to a power supply, whether it's a stand-alone device or built into an alarm control panel, determine the system's power requirements. Equipment specification sheets include current consumption data. Add up the current requirements for all current-consuming devices using the normal, or non-alarm, figures. If the total exceeds 80 percent of the power supply's output, use a larger or additional power supply. The 20 percent margin will be needed when devices go into the alarm state and require additional power.

For example, suppose your panel built-in power supply provides 600mA of auxiliary power. If you connect a wireless receiver, three PIRs and a digital communicator, total normal power consumption might be 400mA. That's under 480mA (80 percent of 600mA).

Adding another power-consuming device, like a motion detector or zone annunciator, will push the total power requirement higher. Although the total still may be less than the 600mA rating, you are entering the overload zone. In this case, a separate 1A power supply should be used. If you anticipate adding more devices later, install a 2A power supply.

Selecting Batteries

Once you have determined a system's power requirements, your next task will be selecting a standby battery. Some manufacturers provide batteries as part of the deal, simplifying the selection process. Others specify the types of batteries to be used with their products. Follow their specifications. If the system requires more power than the recommended battery will deliver, consult the manufacturer before installing a different type or size.

BATTERIES

Because all electronic security systems require power, and because batteries are common components, understanding the types of batteries and their characteristics also helps you understand elementary power-related electronics. In alarm systems, batteries are most often used for standby power, in case AC power fails. A few, usually older, types of systems rely on batteries for primary power.

Various forms of energy, including mechanical, heat, light, and chemical energy, can be converted into electrical energy. Batteries change chemical energy into electrical energy.

Wet Cells

If you combine hydrochloric acid and water, the compound will begin to break down chemically and produce ions, which are electrically charged particles. If you add a strip of zinc and a strip of copper to the acid-and-water solution, and connect the strips with wire, an electrical current will flow between them. The process of producing ions is called *ionization* and the mixture of acid and water is called an *electrolyte*.

The chemical reaction taking place is a result of the zinc and copper strips dissolving in the electrolyte. When the zinc begins to dissolve, it gives up positive ions, thus leaving a surplus of electrons. This creates a negatively charged zinc strip.

As the positive ions float through the electrolyte, they collide with the copper strip. Copper gives up electrons easily. The positive ions neutralize themselves by taking electrons from the copper strip, thus leaving a surplus of protons. This creates a positively charged copper strip.

The difference in electrical charges between the two strips, called *electrodes,* creates an electrical potential, or *voltage.* Placing a conductor, like a piece of wire, between the electrodes allows an electric current to flow between them from negative to positive.

This simple device, consisting of electrodes and an electrolyte, is an electric cell. Because the electrolyte is liquid, it's called a *wet cell.*

This type of cell generates about one volt. The same voltage will be present regardless of whether you have a pint or a gallon of electrolyte. A larger cell, however, allows more current to be drawn from it so it lasts longer and can handle heavier loads.

Dry Cells

The primary cell was developed by Allesandro Volta in about 1800, making him the father of the electrochemical battery. Volta's cell used silver and zinc discs separated by paper or leather wafers which were soaked in an electrolyte.

In the 1860s, Georges Leclanche made significant advancement in battery design when he developed a cell using zinc and manganese dioxide mixed with powdered carbon. The electrolyte was a solution of ammonium chloride dissolved in water. Twenty years later, the liquid electrolyte was reduced to a pasty substance and the *dry cell* was born.

Carbon-Zinc Cells

A typical dry cell uses a carbon rod for the positive electrode and a pasty electrolyte, usually containing ammonia and chlorine. A zinc can surrounds the electrolyte and carbon rod and acts as the negative electrode. Hence, the name *carbon-zinc cell,* commonly referred to as a "flashlight battery."

Most carbon-zinc cells have nominal voltages of 1.5 volts. Like a wet cell, its voltage remains constant and its cell affects the amount of current it can handle. Dry cells have relatively low current-handling capabilities, as shown in Table 8–1.

They also have a limited shelf life. They can go bad even if they are not used. The shelf life of a carbon-zinc cell can be extended if it's stored at temperatures between 40° and 50°F (4° and 10°C). Let them warm to room temperature before using them, however. And, do not freeze carbon-zinc cells because they will have extremely short lives when thawed.

Carbon-zinc cells generate voltage as internal chemicals gradually eat away the negative electrode. Once the electrode is destroyed, the cell is useless. Sometimes cells are useless when they drop below certain voltage levels because the loads they are running will not operate properly below these levels.

Table 8–1.   Typical Current-Handling Capabilities of 1.5V Carbon-Zinc Cells

Size	Current
AAA	20mA
AA	25mA
C	80mA
D	150mA

Voltage remains the same, but current-handling capabilities increase as size increases.

A dying cell can have its life extended somewhat. Apply a small current, with reverse polarity (that is, negative to positive and positive to negative) to it before it dies completely. The recharging current must be kept very small or the reverse polarity will destroy the cell. The requirement for very low current means from 12 to 16 hours of recharging time will be required.

For recharging to be effective, the cell's voltage must not have dropped below 1V (two-thirds of its nominal voltage) and it must be recharged immediately after being removed from service. Moreover, it should be used soon after recharging because it will have a very short shelf life.

Alkaline Cells

Greater current-handling capability is achieved when an alkaline material replaces the acid as the electrolyte. Alkaline cells come in the same sizes as carbon-zinc cells. Table 8–2 shows the typical current available from alkaline cells.

Alkaline cells usually are more expensive than carbon-zinc cells, but they may last five to six times longer in many applications. In the long run, they may be less expensive. In very low current-drain applications, they offer no real advantage because they have a relatively short shelf life.

Table 8–2. Typical Current-Handling Capabilities of 1.5V Alkaline Cells

Size	Current
AAA	200mA
AA	300mA
C	500mA
D	500mA

Like carbon-zinc cells, the larger the alkaline cell, the more current available. More current is available from alkaline cells than from dry cells of the same size, however.

Unlike carbon-zinc cells, alkaline cells cannot be recharged. Attempting to recharge an alkaline cell with reverse polarity current can damage the cell and may cause it to explode.

Nickel-Cadmium Cells

An increasingly popular type of dry cell is the nickel-cadmium cell. These cells can handle moderately large current drains and are rechargeable. Some nickel-cadmium cells can be recharged up to 1,000 times before finally failing.

Most nickel-cadmium cell failures result from voltage dropping too low before recharging. As a general rule, a cell's voltage should not be allowed to drop below 1.05 volts.

Most nickel-cadmium cells produce only 1.25 volts when fully charged, unlike the 1.5 volts produced by fresh carbon-zinc and alkaline cells. Whether or not the .25 volts is significant depends on the device you are powering.

RECHARGEABLE BATTERIES

In many cases, cells are used individually—in a penlight, for example. Combining two or more cells in a common case creates a battery.

Rechargeable batteries are practical and economical for alarm system applications. Their useful life is greater than dry cell batteries because they can be recharged. Although rechargeable batteries cost more, you will save money because you will not have to make service calls as often to replace them. Several types, including nickel-cadmium, lead-acid and gelled electrolyte, are available.

Lead-Acid Batteries

Rechargeable gelled electrolyte lead-acid batteries represent one of the earliest designs for security system use. Many use lead-calcium grids and are vented so the gasses generated during charging can escape.

Sealed rechargeable batteries using pure lead grids also are available. Most sealed batteries last longer than vented ones and their construction helps prevent leaking. Many, depending on construction and manufacturers' specifications, can be installed in any position—even upside down.

Gelled electrolyte batteries are designed to be deep-cycled, deeply discharged and recharged, over long periods of time. They should not be charged or discharged too rapidly.

Cycling energy through gelled electrolyte batteries too quickly can cause gasses to form. They may rupture if gassing occurs in large amounts. If they remain in a discharged state for long periods of time, they are prone to sulphation, the formation of lead sulphate crystals on the cells' plates.

Rate of energy transfer (charging or discharging), type and condition of cell construction, and temperature affect the voltage available at a lead-acid battery's terminals.

Charge and Discharge Rates

To determine a battery's charge or discharge rate, use the following formula:

$$I = C/T$$

where I is the rate of charge (or discharge) expressed in amps, C is the battery's rated capacity expressed in ampere hours, and T is the cycle time period expressed in hours.

SERIES AND PARALLEL CONNECTIONS

Cells can be connected either in series or in parallel. If you need more voltage than a single cell can provide, connect two or more cells in series, as shown in Figure 8–2. Series connections increase voltage but not current output.

If you need more current, connect cells in parallel, as shown in Figure 8–3. Parallel connections increase current but not voltage output.

TIMELY OPERATIONS

Regardless of the battery type, an important consideration is battery operating time. Most battery outputs decrease as temperatures drop. At 32°F, a battery may have only one-half the standby time it has at 72°F. Plan their locations carefully and avoid temperature extremes whenever possible.

Check and replace batteries on a regular schedule. You may want to replace dry cell batteries semi-annually—or annually, at the latest. Rechargeable batteries should be tested annually and replaced every four to five years.

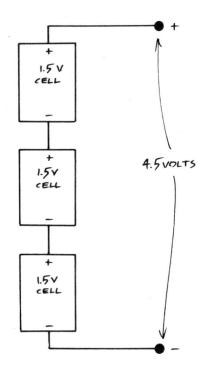

Figure 8–2.   Three 1.5-volt cells connected in series produce 4.5 volts of power output.

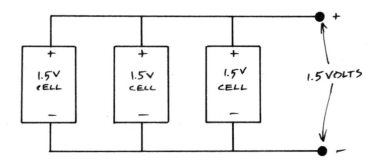

Figure 8–3.   Three 1.5-volt cells connected in parallel produce 1.5 volts of power output.

Adhering to exact replacement schedules is not always possible or practical. Battery life depends on use and a variety of other conditions. Whenever, and for whatever reason, a service call is made, batteries should be checked. To help you develop histories about different types of batteries place labels on the sides of batteries and record replacement and inspection dates and voltage readings.

SHELF LIFE

Batteries lose their charges during storage. Some need recharging every three or six months; others can go three years without recharging. Check your inventory to see how long your batteries have been on your shelves. Then check with your battery supplier to determine how often they should be charged.

While you have your battery supplier on the telephone, ask him these questions:

- What size battery does he recommend for delivering a specific current for a specific length of time—at or above a certain voltage level?
- How much power will the battery deliver at the end of its life?
- How much will it deliver at 0°F?
- How long will the battery last in service?
- What is the battery's yearly service cost? (Battery cost divided by years of service.)
- How long can these batteries be kept in inventory?
- Will stock be fresh when received from supplier?

9

Introduction to Wire and Wiring

Wire may not be the most glamorous component in a security system but it is a necessary one. Almost all security systems require wire. "Wireless" alarm systems just require less wire. For example, wire is needed to connect a wireless control panel to a power source. Wire is needed to connect detection devices, like magnetic contact switches, to transmitters. Hardwired systems require more wire. Large systems may require literally miles of wire.

Selecting the right wire for a job is as important as selecting the proper detection devices and control panel. Knowing the correct wire for an application comes with knowledge and experience. It also requires reading the specifications for a piece of equipment. Equipment manufacturers design their devices to perform in certain ways. To effect correct performance, the devices have certain requirements—one of these requirements often is a specific size and type of wire.

WIRE SIZES

In the United States, wire sizes usually are noted by gauge numbers based on the American Wire Gauge (AWG) system. The larger the AWG number, the smaller the wire and vice versa. Alarm system

93

applications typically use wire ranging from 18- to 22-gauge. For example, 18AWG wire might be needed for connecting a step-down AC transformer or a bell to a control panel. The 22-gauge wire would be used for an alarm system's detection circuits.

You can use larger wire than is necessary. A disadvantage to this is the cost of the wire: larger wire costs more than smaller wire. Using wire that is too small may save you money on the cost of wire, but it could cost you more than what you save.

Copper wire is a good conductor of electricity, but it does offer resistance to power. The resistance in smaller wire is greater than the resistance in larger wire, as shown in Table 9–1. The longer the wire run, the greater the resistance. In circuits providing power, for example, this added resistance will result in a drop in voltage. You might start with 12 volts at the power source, but only 10 volts may be available at the powered device. Depending on the device's operating specifications, 10 volts may be inadequate. The device might operate erratically or not at all. In some cases, running on insufficient power might cause damage.

Table 9–1.   Common Wire Gauges

AWG	Diameter (mils)	Ohms per 1,000 ft. (at 68° F)	Pounds per 1,000 ft.
12	80.808	1.59	19.77
14	64.084	2.52	12.43
16	50.820	4.02	7.82
18	40.303	6.38	4.92
20	31.961	10.15	3.09
22	25.347	16.14	1.94
24	20.100	25.67	1.22
26	15.940	40.81	0.77
28	12.641	64.90	0.48
30	10.025	100.50	0.30
32	7.950	164.10	0.19
34	6.305	260.90	0.12
36	5.000	414.80	0.08

Figure 9–1. Two-conductor insulated wire, commonly called "zip cord," can be used for short power runs.

ALARM WIRE TYPES

Single-conductor insulated wire, usually referred to as *bell wire*, is the simplest type, but has few alarm system uses. Two-conductor insulated wire is more common—either with the two single conductors twisted together (called a *twisted pair*) or run side by side (called *parallel wire* or *zip cord*). Figure 9–1 shows parallel wire.

Most two-conductor wire used by alarm installers is not jacketed. If additional mechanical protection is required, consider using jacketed wire such as the kind shown in Figure 9–2.

The twisting of the wires in a twisted pair affords the wire some shielding from outside interference. Twisted pair with two different colors of insulation helps you identify the individual wires more easily,

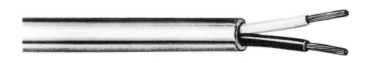

Figure 9–2. Jackets around insulated wires help provide additional protection from the environment and from tampering.

especially in low-light conditions such as often are found in attics. If the wires must be exposed, you probably want the insulation to the same neutral color as the background.

Twisted pair usually has conductors of copper and tinned copper, making them easy to identify. When polarity is important in a circuit, use the copper wire for the positive leg. Use the silver-looking tinned copper conductor for the negative leg.

Two-conductor, insulated parallel wire may have copper and tinned copper conductors as well, but in this case both wires may be copper. If so, the insulation of one of the wires will be ribbed. Use the ribbed side as the positive conductor when polarity must be observed.

Multiple Wires

Four insulated wires inside a common jacket is called a four-conductor, or *quad*, cable. It is the type commonly installed by the telephone company to hook up premise telephone. Telephone company installers usually use 24-gauge wire, which is too small for most alarm system applications. If you are using quad cable for alarm work, be sure it's 22-gauge or larger.

Multi-conductor cables can help save you time and, therefore, money. Plan wiring runs to include strategically located junction boxes for making wiring connections. Run two- or four-conductor cable from detection devices to the junction box, as shown in Figure 9–3. Run a larger multi-conductor cable from the box to the alarm system's control panel.

Be sure to identify and record individual circuits as you connect them to the multi-conductor cable so you can easily identify them when you terminate the cable at the control unit. It is a good idea to label periodically all alarm circuits along wire runs through an attic, basement, or above a suspended ceiling. It will save you time later if you have to troubleshoot the system.

Conductivity

Almost all alarm system wire is made of copper because copper is a good conductor. Silver and gold also are good conductors but are too expensive to be used in wire. The relative conductivity of various conductors is shown in Table 9–2.

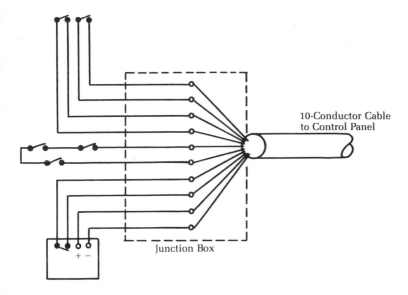

Figure 9–3.   Reduce wiring time by making connections in a junction box and running a single 10-conductor cable to the control panel, instead of using several 2- and 4-conductor cables.

Table 9–2.   Conductivity

Conductor	Relative Conductance
Silver	100
Copper	98
Gold	78
Aluminum	61
Tungsten	32
Zinc	30
Platinum	17
Iron	16

The table shows the relative conductivity of various metals where the conductivity of silver equals 100.

Stranded versus Solid

Whether you use stranded or solid wire depends mostly on the job the wire must do and personal preference, unless specific requirements have been established by local codes, Underwriters Laboratories, or the National Electrical Code (NEC). Conductivity between the same gauges of stranded and solid wire is essentially the same.

There are other considerations, however. If you accidentally nick solid wire while stripping away its insulation, it might break more easily if it is flexed. Nicking or cutting a piece or two of stranded wire, while it should be avoided if possible, probably will not create a serious mechanical or electrical problem.

Solid wire terminates easily and stranded wire offers flexibility. Both types have pros and cons you must consider when selecting wire for a particular job.

Making Connections

The controversy of whether crimping is better than soldering or vice versa, has been going on in the alarm industry for years. No one has a definitive answer. Whether you crimp or solder wire depends partly on preference and partly on where the wire will be installed. The stress the wire might be subjected to should also be considered.

Stranded wire crushes down better than solid wire so crimp-on connectors will hold firmly to it. Crimping tools, like the one shown in Figure 9–4, and the proper pressure help you make good mechanical and electrical connections.

If you are soldering, be sure you get a good solder joint. A cold joint will not provide an adequate electrical-mechanical connection. Clean bare copper thoroughly before soldering. Oil from your fingers or corrosion on the wires may inhibit the flow of solder.

Soldering Tips
- *Use the proper tool.* Soldering irons or guns rated up to 75 watts can be used for most wire. (Use soldering irons or guns rated no larger than 50 watts for soldering electronic components, however.)
- *Tin the tip.* A soldering tool's tip must be cleaned and "tinned" to help provide good heat transfer. Follow the tool manufacturer's instructions to be sure the tip is tinned properly.
- *Prepare the joint.* Make a mechanically strong joint by twisting the

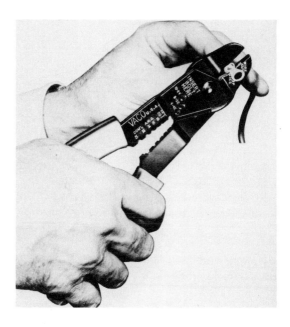

Figure 9–4.   Some wire crimpers can also be used to cut and strip wires. (Photo courtesy of Vaco International.)

wires together so solder will lock and seal the surfaces together. (Solder joints should not depend on the strength of the solder to hold them together.)

- *Heat the parts.* Hold the soldering iron to the joint for a few seconds to preheat the wires. Then add solder. If the solder does not melt, withdraw the solder and apply more heat to the wires.
- *Inspect your work.* A good solder joint is shiny and smooth. A poor ("cold") joint is dull and may be rough.

RUNNING WIRE

Look for channels, ducts and chutes running from one floor to another when planning wire runs. Often, wire can be run next to plumbing vent pipes or heating ducts. Never run wires inside ducts. Keep wires away from heating ducts to prevent melting the insulation and shorting the wires, too.

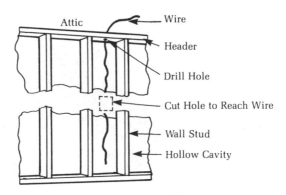

Figure 9–5.   Run wires inside uninsulated interior walls whenever possible.

Locate telephone and low-voltage door bell wires. You may be able
to run alarm wires along the same paths. Never run wires parallel to
high-voltage wires, like 110VAC power circuits. When alarm wires
must cross high-voltage wires, be sure they cross at 90-degree angles.

Interior walls, without insulation, are good for running and concealing wires because they usually do not present many obstructions.
Drill from the attic through the top plate into a wall cavity as shown in
Figure 9–5. After you cut a hole in the wall, you can easily access the
wire or fish tape you dropped into the cavity.

Avoid running wires under carpeting unless no other viable route
exists. If you must run wires under carpets, pull up the carpet where it
meets the wall. Locate the tack strip that holds the carpet in place and
run the wire on the room side of the tack strip. Wires cannot be run
safely over the tack strip because the tacks may puncture and break or
short the wires. Where the wire crosses over the tack strip, remove or
bend down the tacks.

Pull back only a few feet of carpet at a time. After running the wire,
replace the carpet's edge on the tack strip and move along to the
next section.

Another option for running wires is concealing it behind baseboards. In older homes, where baseboards are large and permanent,
this may not be possible. In newer homes, you may be able to gently
pry off the molding, lay the wire behind it, and carefully replace
the molding.

10

Tools and Equipment for Electronics

The right tools make a job simpler and the work proceed faster. Alarm installers' tools range from simple hand tools to sophisticated electronic meters.

Few tools installers use are unique to alarm installations. Drills and screwdrivers are used by many trades. A few other professions may use six-foot-long flexible drill bits, but no other industry uses a special tool to apply foil tape to glass.

BASIC TOOLS

The number and types of tools you will need depend on the types of alarm systems you install. You will need tools to work with sheetrock, paneling, and wood in residential installations. Additional tools for metal and concrete may be required for commercial and industrial installations.

Screwdrivers

Phillips head and standard slot screwdrivers should be readily available in your tool pouch. Phillips head screwdrivers grip screws' heads better than slot screwdrivers. You will need a variety of sizes, blade widths, and thicknesses in both types for tightening both large and small terminals and mounting screws.

Good screwdrivers usually are made from tool steel. They are more expensive than other types, but they will last longer. Plastic handles are more durable than wood ones, too. Rubber-coated handles offer additional comfort.

Make sure the screwdrivers you will be using fit your hand. The handle should be long enough to fit in the palm of your hand. If you cannot get a good grip on the handle, you will have trouble using the screwdriver.

Screwdrivers with detachable heads offer variety without overburdening your tool box or belt. If you opt to go this route, be sure that the blades fit easily, smoothly, and tightly into the handle.

Offset screwdrivers are handy devices when you are working in tight places. They will help you turn screws that cannot be reached easily with an ordinary screwdriver.

Your screwdriver's handle should provide a lot of friction to help you grip the tool. It should not be slippery. A one and one half to two inch diameter handle gives the screwdriver the greatest torque.

Nutdrivers

Nutdrivers are closely related to screwdrivers. A nutdriver has a socket for hex-head screws, instead of a blade. Often it is easier to drive a hex-head screw in tight quarters because the driver does not slip off the screw.

Pliers

Pliers give you the equivalent of a hand with long, strong fingers. Because of the length of their handles, you can exert considerable pressure for holding nuts, wires or other objects.

Pliers come in a variety of sizes and some odd shapes. They also are available with insulated and uninsulated handles. Use the insulated type to help prevent electrical shock and to give you a better grip.

Long-nosed pliers are invaluable for holding small nuts and bolts and working with small wires. They are also useful for bending wires to fit around screw terminals. They can be used in places where fingers cannot or should not go.

Slip-joint pliers usually are larger than long-nosed pliers. They are helpful when working with larger materials, like pieces of sheet metal, flexible tubing and small conduit.

Lineman's pliers combine the features of pliers with wire cutters. They are versatile and useful when you work with 16-gauge wires or larger.

Be sure your pliers' handles are long enough to fit comfortably in your hand and not press into your palm. Short-handled pliers put pressure on the palm where there's less fat. Continued pressure in this area may damage the blood vessels and capillaries under the tendons.

Wrenches

Because the pliers usually are handy, many installers use them for fastening machine nuts. When you do this you must do three things simultaneously: maintain firm pressure on the handles, make sure the jaws have a firm grip on the nut, and apply turning force. This is not impossible, but it is easier to use a wrench to fasten machine nuts; a wrench is designed for this purpose.

Adjustable open-end wrenches are common installation tools. They help you fasten equipment, like space protection devices and cameras, to brackets. You will need several sizes to handle different jobs.

If you work with conduit, you will need a pipe wrench, too. They are made to tighten threaded fastenings on pipe.

Hammers

A good hammer for alarm installers is one made from a continuous piece of steel. A rubber handle will protect you from shock and give you a better grip. You will need a hammer for driving staples, wire rings, and hangers. It is also useful for tapping equipment, like electrical boxes, into position.

Saws

If you install conduit or armored cable, you will need a hacksaw.

Keyhole saws are useful for cutting small pieces of wood and holes in sheetrock.

Wire Fishing Tools

Most alarm installers spend many hours fishing and pulling wires through walls, crawl spaces, attics, and conduit. Fish wire, or fish tape, is a tempered steel spring about one-fourth inch wide and available in various lengths. Flat, wide tapes also are available.

This stiff wire lets you push or pull wire through straight openings. It is also flexible enough to let you maneuver wires through bends and elbows in conduit.

A drop chain, small chain lengths attached to a lead or iron weight, helps simplify running wires, too. It is used to feed wires through vertical openings.

Drills

Portable electric hand drills are common alarm installation tools. You can buy a drill that only drills—rotating in one direction at a single speed. A more useful tool for alarm installers is a variable speed drill with a reversing switch.

A variable speed drill lets you begin drilling from a standstill with-

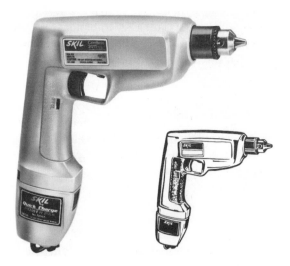

Figure 10–1. Cordless drill–screwdriver combinations make many installation tasks easier. (Photo courtesy of Skil Corp.)

out having your bit shift. Use high speeds for drilling soft woods; slower speeds provide more torque for drilling metal and concrete.

A reversible drill helps you remove the bit after drilling a hole. You can withdraw bits, especially the long, flexible ones, and pull wires out of the hole easier when they rotate backwards.

Cordless drill-screwdriver combinations, like the one shown in Figure 10–1, also are useful. They let you drill and drive screws in places where dragging an extension cord would be difficult.

Check your drill's trigger. You should be able to press it with the middle joint of your finger and not just with the joint at the tip. The drill's handle should be small enough to fit your hand comfortably.

Staple Guns

A staple gun, like the one shown in Figure 10–2, is one of the most indispensable tools an alarm installer uses. Without it, you would have

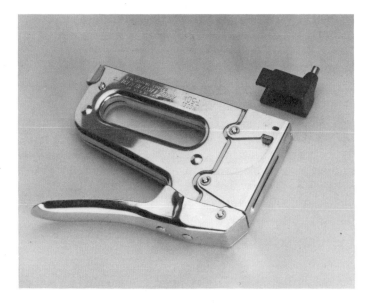

Figure 10–2.   Staple guns allow you to attach wires to beams and walls. With special attachments, you can shoot fasteners into wood and masonry. (Photo courtesy of Arrow Fastener Co., Inc.)

difficulty running wires and keeping them out of harm's way. Some staple guns have attachments, like the one shown, that also allow you to perform other tasks like driving special fasteners in wood and masonry.

Wire Strippers and Cutters

Wire strippers have a series of different-sized holes in their blades for cutting through and removing the insulation around different gauges of wire. Experienced installers strip wires with a variety of items, including jackknives and diagonal cutters. It takes a lot of practice to cut only through insulation without nicking wires. Unless you are very good at it, use wire strippers to save time and wire.

Diagonal cutters, often called "dikes" or "side cuts," are designed for cutting wire. A slot for stripping wire is a useful feature found on some models. Do not use the tool to cut hard metals, like nails and screws, because you will nick and damage the tool's cutting face.

Special multipurpose wire tools let you cut and strip wires. They usually have a section for crimping wire connectors, too (see Figure 9–4).

Soldering Tools

Soldering tools, including irons, pencils and guns, are available in a variety of sizes, shapes, and wattage rating. Most electronics work requires soldering tools rated at less than 50 watts.

Cordless soldering irons are handy items for the alarm installer's tool box. They are powered by rechargeable batteries and can be moved from place to place easily. They are not designed for extended use, however, so if you will be soldering a lot of connections, you may need an electric soldering iron.

TEST EQUIPMENT

Alarm installers and service technicians often find it necessary to measure various properties of circuits; ammeters are used for measuring current, voltmeters for voltage, and ohmmeters for resistance. The most useful meter for most field work is a multitester—sometimes called a volt-ohm-milliammeter and abbreviated VOM. It is a single instrument for measuring voltage, resistance and current.

Most meters are available in analog and digital versions. If you need precise measurements, select a digital meter. Digital units are more expensive and if you tend to misplace or lose them, the less expensive analog meters should be your choice. Analog meters work well for most field tasks.

General Precautions

Protect your meter from magnetic fields. Prolonged exposure to magnetism may adversely affect your meter's operation.

Carry an extra set of leads in your tool box. If the leads you are using become damaged, throw them away. Check the leads if your meter begins giving you faulty or erratic readings.

Every time you use your meter, check that it is operating properly. Be sure the battery is charged and the meter's leads are not loose or frayed.

Ammeters

Electric current is measured with an ammeter—a shortened form of ampere meter. Because an ampere usually is too large for alarm system circuits, milliammeters or microammeters are used frequently. All three meters work the same way, differing only in the range of values they are capable of measuring.

In a series circuit the current is equal at all points, so if an ammeter is placed in series with the rest of the circuit, the same current that flows through the circuit will flow through the meter.

Voltmeters

A voltmeter measures voltage. Like the ammeter, it is placed in series with the circuit being tested.

If you are comparing voltages between two similar circuits, the meters used in each circuit should have the same internal resistance— or you should use the same meter. If meters with different internal resistances are used, you may obtain different readings from the same voltage levels.

Ohmmeters

A common type of meter used by alarm installers and technicians measures direct current (DC) resistance and is called an ohmmeter.

You do not have to do any calculations to use an ohmmeter because the scale is calibrated to read the resistance directly in ohms.

Volt-Ohm-Milliammeters

A volt-ohm-milliammeter (VOM) is an indispensable testing device. It measures voltage and resistance. Small VOMs are most useful in the field where they can be used to verify voltage levels and check open and closed circuits. The scale face of a VOM usually has several calibration markings so each metering function can be read directly.

MISCELLANEOUS TOOLS, EQUIPMENT AND SUPPLIES

Numerous other indispensable items are found in an alarm installer's tool box or pouch. Some are readily available through hardware and electrical supply stores, some are homemade devices.

Electrical Tape

Current-carrying wires are insulated; otherwise the current could seek a shorter path and cause a short circuit. When you strip away the insulating material for wiring connections, you create a potential pathway for a short. Electrical tape supplies insulating protection for these connections.

Plastic or vinyl electrical tape has a long life span and is flexible enough to wrap wires tightly. For added protection, wrap the wires twice. The object of a tape wrap is to make a tight covering, not a large lump. Tightness improves the effectiveness of the adhesive's holding power.

If you buy a large stock of electrical tape, store rolls in a sealed container until you are ready to use them. Keeping the tape in a sealed container helps keep it fresh.

Electrical Boxes

Electrical boxes provide convenient points for wire splices. They are available in rectangular, square, and octagonal shapes. Special splice boxes have tamper switches to tell you if a cover has been removed.

Table 10–1. Extension Cord Wire Sizes

Ampere rating:	Up to 2	2.1–3.4	3.5–5.0	5.1–7.0	7.1–12
Extension cord length (in feet)	Minimum wire size (AWG)				
25	18	18	18	18	16
50	18	18	18	16	14
75	18	18	16	14	12
100	18	16	14	12	10
150	16	14	12	12	—
200	16	14	12	10	—

Extension cords that are too small for the job may damage your electric tools. Be sure to select the proper size for the tool's amperage and distance from the power source.

Extension Cords

Selecting the proper extension cord will help avoid damaging your electrical tools and blowing fuses or tripping circuit breakers. Table 10–1 shows the minimum wire size for extension cords of various lengths and for various loads your tool places on the circuit. If the tool you are using is rated in watts instead of amps, then divide watts by volts. (The result is the tool's amperage rating.)

Solder

The most commonly used solder alloy contains 60 percent lead and 40 percent tin and usually is referred to as "60/40" solder. The melting temperature of 60/40 solder is low enough to allow safe soldering of most heat-sensitive electronic components. Most modern solders for electronics have a core of rosin flux that automatically cleans away oxides during soldering.

Solder is available in a variety of types and sizes. Once you select the appropriate type, consider the size you will need. For most electronics work, the best size to use is about 30 gauge.

11

Safety Considerations

Good safety precautions not only protect you from injury or death, they also help protect security equipment and your customer's property from damage. Electric shock is one of the most common hazards encountered by alarm installers and service technicians.

"High voltage kills" is a good statement to remember. Touching a 10,000 volt power line certainly can kill you. Because you are working with "low" voltages, usually 117VAC from the primary power source and no higher than 24 volts from the secondary source, do not assume you are safe.

Voltage is only one of the factors in the degree of shock you receive. Household voltages of 110 to 120VAC can kill. Deaths have been recorded from much lower voltages.

How badly you will be shocked depends on:

1. The amount of current, measured in milliamperes, that flows through your body.
2. The path the current takes through your body.
3. The time, in milliseconds, you are exposed to the shock.

Other factors affecting your ability to withstand electric shock include your age, size, and physical condition.

Your body offers some resistance to electricity, just as wires and other components offer resistance to the flow of electricity. The amount of resistance in your body varies from about 300 ohms to more than 100,000 ohms, depending on the point of electrical contact, skin thickness, callouses, perspiration, and the path the current takes. About 500 ohms is the maximum resistance you can count on. At 500 ohms, 9 volts is the most you can touch safely.

For you to receive a shock, you must be part of a closed circuit through which electricity can flow. If your body's resistance is 100,000 ohms, about 1mA will flow through you if you grab both ends of a 117VAC circuit. Most people voluntarily let go when they feel the shock.

Current increases as resistance decreases. You will probably feel between 1 and 6mA as a "tingle." In such an instance, death probably would not be a direct result of the electrical shock. You might be startled and fall from a ladder, however.

AC currents above 6mA can be deadly. At 25mA muscles can go into violent contractions. Between 25 and 200mA, the current can throw your heart out of rhythm or your breathing may stop.

Safe "let-go" currents are 9mA for men and 6mA for women. If you are connected to circuits above these levels, serious consequences can result.

If current flow is of very short duration, exposure to it may not be serious or fatal. That is why ground-fault interruptors (GFIs), like the one shown in Figure 11-1 are important safety tools. These devices typically allow current to flow for no more than 25 milliseconds.

The path current takes can affect the severity of the shock you receive. If it flows from one finger to another on the same hand it will be less severe than if it flows from one hand through your heart and lungs to the other hand. If you are working on a "hot" circuit, put one hand behind your back or in your pocket.

DUMB MOVES

Here are some shock hazards that should be avoided at all costs:

- Frayed or broken electrical cords.
- Testing a circuit with your finger to see if it is live.
- Working on circuits you assume to be off, but have not checked.

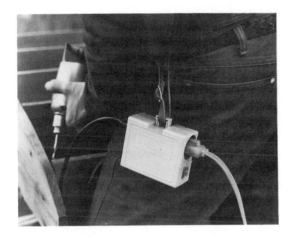

Figure 11–1. Ground–fault interrupters help protect you from hazardous shocks and possible electrocution while working with electrical tools.

- Working on circuits that could be turned on accidentally by others.
- Any electrical device that gives you a "tingle" when you touch it.
- All electrical tools that do not have a U.L. label.
- Ungrounded tools (unless they are double insulated).

SAFE PRACTICES

When working with electronic components and wires, keep these tips in mind.

- When electrical conductors are joined by splicing, the connection must be strong and safe, and must provide a path for the continuous flow of electricity.
- Soldered splices must first be properly joined mechanically before soldering.
- All splices and free ends of conductors must be covered with an insulation that will withstand the same environmental conditions and voltages as the original conductors. Suitable insulation for most alarm system conductors includes electrical tape, end caps, and heat-shrink tubing.

STATIC ELECTRICITY

Static electricity is more of a nuisance than a hazard for most people. The jolts may be uncomfortable and annoying, but they probably will not kill you.

That is not the case for electronic equipment, however. Static electricity can "kill" a control panel, for example. Or, if it does not kill it, it may cause it to operate erratically. A small static spark may contain tens of thousands of volts.

Alarm components' circuit boards are very sensitive. Always ground yourself to help prevent damaging the equipment by static electricity discharges from your body. Your body may contain thousands of volts of electricity, especially in cool, dry weather. Even a tiny spark can severely damage microprocessor-based circuits.

LADDERS

Ladder accidents are some of the easiest to prevent. Falls, even from heights of less than 10 feet, can cause severe injury or death.

When you purchase a ladder, be sure it conforms to the standards of either the American National Standards Institute (ANSI) or Underwriters Laboratories (UL).

Aluminum ladders are lighter than wooden ones, but they can be deadly around power lines. Fiberglass ladders are the most durable.

Table 11–1. Heights for Extension Ladders

Height to reach	Length of Ladder
9.5 feet	16 feet
13.5 feet	20 feet
17.5 feet	24 feet
21.5 feet	28 feet
24.5 feet	32 feet
29.0 feet	36 feet

The maximum working length of an extension ladder is not as great as its total length because of overlapping sections and the angle at which the ladder must be placed.

They will stand up to weather, and will not conduct electricity, splinter or rot.

Select a ladder that is long enough for expected uses. Working on a ladder's top rungs or steps is dangerous. Table 11–1 shows suggested lengths for extension ladders to allow you to reach different heights.

Set an extension ladder at the proper distance from the wall on which you are working. The bottom of the ladder should be one fourth of the vertical height away from the wall. For example, for a vertical height of 16 feet, the base of the ladder should be four feet from the wall.

Table 11–2. Noise Levels

Item/Event/Area	Noise Level (dB)
Carrier deck jet operation	150
Jet takeoff (200 feet)	120
Discotheque	115
Alarm siren	110
New York subway station	95
Pneumatic drill (50 feet)	85
Vacuum cleaner	80
Alarm clock	80
Garbage disposal	80
Freight train (50 feet)	75
Freeway traffic (50 feet)	70
Coffee grinder	70
Portable 1/4-inch drill	70
Conversation (average)	45
Living room	40
Soft whisper	30
Broadcasting studio	20
(Just audible)	10
(Threshold of hearing)	0

Normal conversation is difficult to carry on against background noise of 60dB and almost impossible against background noise of 70dB. You have to shout to be heard above 90dB background noise. Hearing impairment can begin at sound levels as low as 80dB if exposure is prolonged.

NOISE

Noise is dangerous in two ways. First, loud ambient noises may prevent you from hearing lower noises or co-workers signaling danger. Second, prolonged exposure to loud noises causes stress and may damage your hearing. Table 11–2 shows typical noise levels for various events. Table 11–3 shows permissible noise exposures established by the Occupational Safety and Health Administration (OSHA).

WEATHER

Safety concerns extend beyond buildings' perimeters. Weather factors also can affect safety.

Lightning

Lightning is one of nature's most beautiful displays—if you are viewing it from a distance. In a split second, a lightning bolt exceeding 100,000,000 volts can streak between clouds, or between the earth and a cloud.

The peak current in one of these thunderous bursts may exceed 200,000 amps. If the bolt is near you it can electrocute you and crush any structure that becomes part of its path.

Table 11–3.   Permissible Noise Exposure

Ambient Noise Level (dB)	Exposure Duration (Hours per Day)
90	8
92	6
95	4
97	3
100	2
102	1.5
105	1
110	0.5
115	0.25

Prolonged exposure to high ambient noise levels can cause hearing damage.

Table 11–4.   Wind Chill Factor Comparisons

Wind Velocity	Calm	15 mph	30 mph	40 mph
Temperature (°F)	30	11	− 2	− 4
	20	− 6	− 18	− 22
	10	−18	− 33	− 36
	0	−33	− 49	− 54
	−10	−45	− 63	− 69
	−20	−60	− 78	− 87
	−30	−70	− 94	−101
	−40	−85	−109	−116

Cold temperatures can numb senses and make normally safe procedures dangerous.

It is estimated that lightning strikes the earth about 100 times per second, generated from the 1,500 to 2,000 thunderstorms in progress at any given time. This information alone should be enough to make you stop working on an alarm system during a thunderstorm.

Wind and Temperature

If you are working outside, remember that wind aloft may be stronger than wind on the ground. It may be windier and colder at the top of a tower or on the roof of a building than at lower elevations.

Wind chill is a serious factor. It numbs senses and makes working efficiently and safely difficult. Table 11–4 shows wind chill factors at various temperatures and wind velocities.

Security Electronics Glossary

A 1. Ampere. 2. Area.

AC Alternating current

AC line A power line delivering alternating current only.

AC line carrier A system that transmits signals over standard AC power lines.

AC line voltage The voltage commonly delivered by a commercial power line to a consumer. In the United States, AC line voltage usually is 110 to 120 volts. In Europe, 220V is common.

AC noise Electrical noise of a rapidly alternating or pulsating nature.

AC power supply A power unit, like a generator, which supplies AC power. (Compare *DC power supply.*)

AC relay A relay designed to operate on alternating current without vibrating.

AC voltage A voltage which alternates, or periodically changes, its polarity from negative to positive to negative, and so forth.

Ah or Ah Ampere-hour.

alkaline battery A battery composed of alkaline cells.

alkaline cell A primary cell in which the negative electrode is granular zinc mixed with a potassium hydroxide (alkaline) electrolyte, and the positive electrode is a polarizer in electrical contact with the outer metal can of the cell.

Figure A–1.   Alligator clip.

alligator clip   A clip lead with jagged teeth, designed to be used with temporary electrical connections (see Figure A–1).
alternating current (AC)   A current which periodically alternates its direction of flow, switching rapidly from negative to positive to negative, and so forth.
ambient temperature   Temperature of the surrounding medium, usually air, in a specified area.
American Wire Gauge (AWG)   The standard American method of designating the various wire sizes. Wire is listed according to gauge numbers ranging from 0000 to 40. The larger the number, the smaller the wire. Also called Brown and Sharpe or B&S gauge.
ammeter   An instrument used for measuring the amount of current (amperes) flowing in a circuit.
amp   Common verbal abbreviation for ampere. (Also see *A* and *ampere.*)
ampacity   Current-carrying capacity expressed in amperes.
amperage   The strength (number of amperes) of an electric current.
ampere (A or amp)   The SI base unit of current intensity (I). One ampere flows through one ohm of resistance when a potential of 1 volt is applied; thus, $I = E/R$ (Ohm's law). Named for André-Marie Ampère, 1775–1836.
ampere-hour   The quantity of electricity that passes through a circuit in one hour when the rate of flow is one ampere.
ampere's law   Current flowing in a wire generates a magnetic flux which encircles the wire in the clockwise direction when the current is moving away from the observer.
amp-hr   Ampere-hour. (Also see *AH.*)
Analog   Representation of data by continuously variable quantities.
analog meter   An indicating instrument with values along a graduated scale. (Compare *digital meter.*)
angle of incidence   The angle made by a ray and the perpendicular to the surface struck by the ray.

angle of reflection   The angle made by a ray and the perpendicular to the surface the ray leaves.

anneal   To heat metal to a specific temperature and then let it cool slowly. The operation prevents brittleness and helps stablize electrical characteristics.

annealed wire   Soft-drawn wire that has undergone annealing.

annealing   The removal of metal hardness by heating it to approximately 1,000°F, and then allowing it to cool very slowly.

anode   The positive electrode of a device, making it the electrode toward which electrons move during current flow.

ANSI   American National Standards Institute.

antioxidant   A material, like a lacquer coat, that prevents or slows oxidation of a substance exposed to air.

applied voltage   The voltage presented to a circuit point or system input, as opposed to the voltage drop resulting from current flow through an element.

armor   A braid or wrapping of metal, usually steel or aluminum, around wires for mechanical protection.

AWG   American wire gauge.

backup battery   Reserve power source in case of primary (AC) power failure.

balanced cable   A cable with two inner conductors of the same diameter that are insulated from each other. The two conductors are surrounded by additional insulation and a coaxial-type shield. These 124-ohm cables offer advantages for long runs because they help eliminate hum and grounding problems.

bandpass   A specific range of frequencies that will pass through a device. For example, video systems usually pass 30Hz to 6 MHz.

bandpass filter   A filter that will allow to pass only a specific frequency band.

bare conductor   A conductor, usually wire, having no insulating covering.

barrier strip   A terminal strip with non-conducting barriers between terminals (see Figure A–2).

BAT   Battery. Also abbreviated B and BA.

bat-handle switch   A toggle switch with a relatively long lever shaped similarly to a baseball bat.

battery   A multicell electrochemical device that generates DC electricity. A battery consists of a group of cells connected in series to supply a desired voltage, in parallel to supply a desired current, or both.

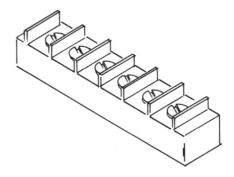

Figure A–2.   Barrier strip.

battery back-up   See *backup battery.*

battery capacity   The current-supplying capability of a battery, usually expressed in ampere-hours (AH).

battery charger   A DC power supply used to charge a storage battery from an AC power line.

battery life   1. The ampere-hour or watt-hour capacity of a battery. 2. The number of times a rechargeable battery can be cycled before it becomes unusable.

bench test   An extensive examination of a piece of equipment in a shop or laboratory, either to find an intermittent problem or to check for reliability.

bimetal   A union of two dissimilar metals.

bimetallic element   A strip or disk of bimetal. When heated, the element bends in the direction of the metal having the lower temperature coefficient of expansion; when cooled, it straightens. In some devices, like heat detectors, an electrical contact is made at one extreme or the other.

bimetallic switch   A temperature-sensitive switch based upon a bimetallic element.

binary   A numbering system using 2 as its base (10 is the base used in the decimal system). The binary system uses two symbols—0 and 1. Most alarm system devices are based on binary codes. For example, on-off and high-low show binary (two-condition) relationships.

binary code   A system of numbers, representing quantities, that uses combinations of 0 and 1.

bit In the binary system, the smallest unit of information, consisting of a 0 or a 1. The word is formed from *b*inary dig*it*.

body capacitance Capacitance between the body of the operator and a piece of electronic equipment that sometimes causes detuning or interference.

braided wire A length of braid often used for grounding or shielding.

breakdown voltage (BV) 1. The voltage at which current suddenly passes through a dielectric in destructive amounts. 2. The voltage at which the reverse current of a semiconductor junction suddenly rises to a high value (nondestructive if the current is limited).

burn-in The preliminary operation of a device to help stabilize its electrical characteristics after manufacture.

bus 1. Wires or cables interconnecting system components. 2. A common return path for electrical or electronic circuits. 3. A collection of wires for parallel data transmission.

BV Breakdown voltage.

bypass A path (either intended or accidental) through which current flows around a component or circuit instead of through it.

byte A group of adjacent binary digits (8 bits).

C 1. Capacitance. 2. Collector of a transistor. 3. Carbon. 4. Celsius. 5. Coulomb.

cable A group of individually insulated conductors in twisted or parallel configuration contained in a common sheath.

cable assembly A special-purpose cable with connectors.

cable clamp A support device for holding cable.

cable connector A connector, such as a coaxial fitting, that joins cable circuits or connects a cable to a device.

cable coupler A device to join lengths of similar or dissimilar cables having the same electrical characteristics.

cable run The path along which a cable is installed.

calibrate To compare and align with a standard.

calibrated meter An analog or digital meter that has been adjusted to agree as closely as possible with a reference source.

can A metal enclosure or container.

cap 1. Capacitance. 2. Capacitor.

capacitance Symbol, C. Unit, farad. The property exhibited by two conductors separated by a dielectric, whereby an electric charge becomes stored betwen the conductors.

capacitor A passive electronic-circuit component usually consisting of two metal electrodes or plates separated by a dielectric (insulator).

capacitor leakage   Direct current flowing through the dielectric of a capacitor. In a good nonelectrolytic capacitor this current may be less than 1 microampere. In an electrolytic capacitor, it may be several milliamperes.

capacity   1. A measure of a cell or battery's ability to supply current during a given period. 2. The number of bits or bytes a computer storage device can hold.

cathode   The negative electrode of a device. (Compare *anode*.)

cell   A single unit for producing DC electricity by electrochemical or biochemical action.

Celsius scale   A temperature scale in which zero is the freezing point of water, and 100, the boiling point of water.

charge   1. A quantity of electricity associated with a space, particle, or body. 2. To electrify a space, particle, or body, that is, to give an electric charge. 3. To store electricity, as in a storage battery or capacitor.

charging   The process of storing electrical energy in a battery or a capacitor.

charging current   The current flowing into a battery or capacitor.

charging rate   1. The rate at which charging current flows into a battery, expressed in ampere-hours or milliampere-hours. 2. The rate at which charging current flows into a capacitor or capacitance-resistance circuit, expressed in amperes, milliamperes, or microamperes.

chip   A small slab, wafer, or die of dielectric or semiconductor material on which a subminiature or microminiature component or circuit is formed. (See *integrated circuit*.)

choke   To restrict or stop passage of a particular current or frequency by means of a discrete component, such as a choke coil.

choke coil   An inductor providing high impedance to alternating current while offering virtually no opposition to direct current.

circuit   A complete path in which electrons can flow. In alarm systems, a circuit begins with the negative terminal of a voltage source, continues through wire and protective devices' contacts and terminates at the positive terminal of the same source.

circuit board   A panel, plate, or card on which components are mounted and interconnected to create a functional device.

circuit breaker   A resettable fuse-like device designed to help protect a circuit against overloading.

circuit, closed   1. An electrical circuit in which current normally flows until interrupted by the opening of a switch or switch-type electronic component. 2. A circuit in which contacts are closed during normal operation. Opening the circuit triggers an alarm. Also called a normally closed (NC) circuit. 3. A protective circuit consisting of all normally closed devices connected in series. A break in the circuit or activation of one or more sensors triggers an alarm.

circuit diagram   A drawing with symbols and lines representing components and wires in an electronic circuit.

circuit, open   1. An electrical circuit in which current does not flow until permitted by the closing of a switch, or a switch-type electronic component. 2. A circuit in which contacts are open during normal operation. Closing the circuit triggers an alarm. Also called a normally open (NO) circuit.

circuit tester   An instrument for checking electronic circuits. (Also see *multimeter.*)

circular mil   The area of a circle having a diameter of 0.001 inch. The term is used to specify the cross-sectional area of a wire.

clip   A connector whose jaws are normally held closed by a spring.

closed circuit   See *circuit, closed.*

CMOS   Complementary metal-oxide semiconductor.

coaxial cable   A cable consisting of two concentric conductors—an inner wire and an outer braided sleeve—capable of passing a wide range of frequencies with very low signal loss. Most coaxial cables have a 75-ohm impedance. Often referred to as "coax" (see Figure A–3).

coaxial connector   A device used for splicing coaxial cable or connecting a coaxial cable to a piece of equipment or device (see Figure A–4).

cold solder joint   A solder joint in which insufficient heat has been applied, resulting in a bad connection. Cold solder joints usually have a dull appearance, while good (hot) joints are shiny.

color code   A system using colored markings to indicate the nominal

Figure A–3.   Coaxial cable.

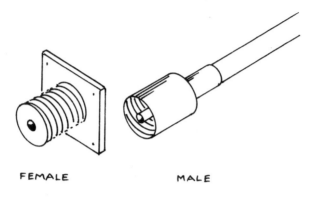

FEMALE   MALE

Figure A–4.   Coaxial connector.

values and other characteristics on capacitors, resistors, and other components.

common   1. A point utilized by several components or wires. 2. Directly connected to several different points in a circuit or system. 3. Sometimes used as the shortened form of "common ground." (See *ground, common*.)

complementary metal-oxide semiconductor (CMOS)   A semiconductor device consisting of two complementary MOSFETs (that is, one n-channel type and one p-channel type) integrated into a single chip.

component   A device or part employed in a circuit to obtain some desired electrical action.

conductance   Symbol, G. Unit, siemens. The ability of a circuit, conductor, or device to conduct electricity. The reciprocal of resistance. $G = 1/R = I/E$.

conduction   1. The transfer of electrons through a wire or other conductor. 2. Heat transfer through an object.

conductivity   The capability of a material to carry electrical current, usually expressed as a percentage of copper conductivity (copper being 100 percent conductive).

conductor   1. A material, like copper wire, which conducts electricity with ease. (Compare *insulator*.) 2. An individual conducting wire in a cable.

conduit   A tube or trough in which insulated wires and cables are run.

connect   To provide an electrical path between two points.

connection   The point at which two conductors meet.

connector   Any device providing electrical connection.

contact   1. A conducting body—like a button, disk, or blade—that, upon touching another conductor, serves to close an electric circuit (for example, switch contact, spring contact) 2. The state of being touched together, as when two conductors are brought into contact to close a circuit.

contact rating   The maximum current, voltage, or power specified for a given set of contacts.

contact resistance   The amount of resistance (usually very low) in the closed contacts of switches, relays, and similar devices.

contact switch   A switch which uses a contact (see *contact*, 1) to make and break an electric circuit, as compared with an electronic switch, which uses the on-off action of a bistable tube or transistor.

continuity   State of being complete and uninterrupted, like a normally closed detection circuit.

continuous circuit   An uninterrupted circuit. A closed circuit.

continuous duty   The requirement of a device to sustain a 100 percent duty cycle for a prolonged period of time.

continuous-duty rating   The maximum current, voltage, or power rating for a device operated for extended periods.

copper (**Cu**)   A metallic element. Atomic number, 29. Atomic weight, 63.54. Copper is a good conductor of electricity and heat.

cps   1. Cycles per second. To denote AC frequency, cycles per second is referred to as hertz (Hz). 2. Characters per second.

Cu   Symbol for copper.

current   Symbol, I. The flow of electricity, that is, the movement of electrons through a conductor. $I = E/R$. (Also see *ampere* and *Ohm's law*.)

current-carrying capacity   The maximum current (usually expressed in amperes) that a conductor or device can safely conduct.

current drain   1. The current supplied to a load (device) from a power source. 2. The current required by a device for its operation.

current flow   Current passing through a solid, liquid, gas, or vacuum.

d   Deci.

dB or **db**   Decibel.

DC   Direct current.

DC source   1. DC generator. 2. A live circuit from which one or more direct currents can be taken.

DCV   DC volts or DC voltage.

DC voltage (DCV)   A voltage which does not change in polarity, such as the voltage delivered by a battery or DC generator. (Also see *voltage*.)

DC working voltage (DCWV)   The rated DC voltage at which a component may be operated continuously, safely, and reliably.

DC working volts (DCWV)   The actual value, expressed in volts, of a DC working voltage.

DCWV   DC working volts or DC working voltage.

dead short   A short circuit having extremely low (or virtually no) resistance.

Deca   A prefix meaning ten; for example, decagram.

deci (d)   A prefix meaning one tenth, that is, 10^{-1}.

decibel (dB or db)   A measurement used to compare measured levels of sound energy (intensity) to the apparent level detected by the human ear, expressed as a logarithmic ratio. A sound having 10 times the energy of another is said to be 10 decibels louder; 100 times the energy, 20 decibels louder; 1,000 times the energy, 30 decibels louder, and so on. Correctly expressed as the number of decibels at a measured distance from the course of sound (for example, 125 dB at 10 feet).

deg   Degree.

degree   1. A unit of circular measurement equal to 1/360 the circumference of a circle. Also called geometric degree. 2. A unit of temperature measurement (for example, degrees Celsius and degrees Fahrenheit).

deka   A prefix meaning ten, that is, 10^1.

delay contacts   Contacts that open or close at a predetermined instant after their activating signal is applied or removed.

delay relay   A relay that opens or closes at the end of a predetermined time interval.

delay timer   A timer that starts or stops an operation after a prescribed length of time. In some senses, a delay relay or delay contacts.

denominator   The term below or to the right of the division of a fraction. The denominator is the divisor in a fraction representing division. (Compare *numerator*.)

desolder   To unsolder joints, especially with a special tool which protects delicate parts and removes the melted solder by suction.

dielectric   Any insulating material between two conductors which permits electrostatic attraction and repulsion to take place across it.

digital meter   An indicating instrument in which a row of numeral indicators displays a value. (Compare *analog meter.*)

diode   A device that contains an anode and a cathode (as a tube) or a pn junction (as a semiconductor device) as principal elements and that provides unidirectional conduction.

DIP   Dual-inline package.

dip soldering   1. Soldering leads or terminals by dipping them into molten solder and then removing excess solder. 2. Tinning printed-circuit patterns by dipping the printed-circuit boards into molten solder or placing them in contact with the surface of a solder bath. Also, soldering leads in printed circuits by the same methods.

DIP switch   A switch (or group of miniature switches) mounted in a dual-inline package for easy insertion into an integrated-circuit socket or printed-circuit board (see Figure A–5).

direct current (DC)   Electrical current that travels in one direction and has negative (−) and positive (+) polarity. Primary AC power usually is converted to DC power to operate alarm equipment. Batteries are DC power sources that supply secondary, or standby, power to alarm systems.

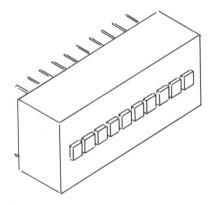

Figure A–5.   DIP switch.

direction of current flow   Electron drift from a negative point to a positive point. Because the drift is the basis of current flow, current is said to flow from negative to positive.

discharge   The emptying or draining of electricity from a source, such as a battery or capacitor. The term also denotes a sudden, heavy flow of current, as in disruptive discharge. (Compare *charge*.)

discharge current   1. Current flowing out of a capacitor. 2. Current flowing out of a cell, especially a storage cell. (Compare *charging current*.)

discharge rate   The current which can be supplied by a battery reliably over a given period. Expressed in milliamperes, amperes, milliampere-hours, or ampere-hours.

disconnect   1. To separate connections, thereby interrupting a circuit. 2. A type of connector whose halves may be pulled apart to open a cable or other circuit quickly.

disk capacitor   A fixed (usually two-plate) capacitor consisting of a disk of dielectric material on whose faces are deposited metal-film plates (see Figure A–6).

dissipation   The consumption of power, often without contributing to a useful end and usually accompanied by the generation of heat.

distributive law   The arithmetic law stating x(y + z) is the equivalent of xy + xz.

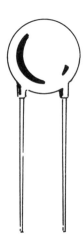

Figure A–6.   Disk capacitor.

DMM or dmm   Digital multimeter.

DOM or dom   Digital ohmmeter.

doohickey   A usually unnamed device, especially one used to achieve some significant modification of circuit performance. Also often referred to as a gadget.

double-circuiting   Using redundant wires to connect all sensors in an alarm system.

double-pole   Having two poles (for example, a double-pole switch).

double-pole, double-throw switch or relay (DPDT)   A switch or relay having two contacts which may be operated simultaneously in one of two directions to close or open two circuits.

double-pole, single-throw switch or relay (DPST)   A switch or relay having two poles which may be operated in one direction to simultaneously close or open two circuits.

double shield   Two independent electromagnetic shields for a circuit enclosure or cable. The shielding structures are concentric, and may be connected together at a single point (the common point) (see Figure A–7).

double-throw   Operating in opposite directions, as selected (for example, a double-throw relay or switch).

double-throw switch or relay   A switch or relay having two ganged poles. (see *double-pole, double-throw switch or relay* and *double-pole, single-throw switch or relay.*)

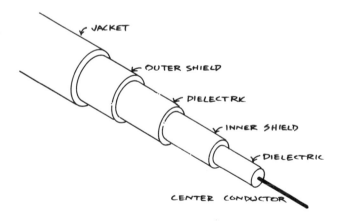

Figure A–7.   Double shield.

DPDT   Double-pole, double-throw (switch or relay).

DPST   Double-pole, single-throw (switch or relay).

drain   The current or power drawn from a signal or other source.

drop relay   In a telephone system, a relay that is activated by the ringing signal. The relay is used to switch on a buzzer, light, or other device.

dry battery   A battery comprised of dry cells.

dry cell   1. A Leclanche primary cell in which the positive electrode is carbon; the negative electrode, zinc; and the electrolyte, a gel of ammonium chloride and additives. (Also see *cell* and *primary cell*.) 2. A battery cell whose electrolyte is a gel or paste.

dry circuit   A circuit in which the maximum voltage is 50 mV and the maximum current 200 mA.

dry contact   Metallic points making (shorting) or breaking (opening) a circuit. Electrical connection points provided in a circuit or system for switching external circuits, but electrically isolated from the controlling circuit. The externally switched circuit must have its own source of power, and is merely routed through the dry contacts.

dry-reed switch   A switch consisting of two thin, metallic strips (reeds) hermetically sealed in a glass tube. When an external magnet is brought close by, it attracts one of the reeds, which then contacts the other reed, closing the circuit (see Figure A–8).

dual-inline package (**DIP**)   A flat, molded IC package having terminal lugs along both long edges.

DVM or dvm   Digital voltmeter.

DVOM or dvom   Digital volt-ohm-milliammeter.

E   1. Voltage. 2. Electric field strength. 3. Emitter.

EEPROM   Electrically erasable programmable read-only memory. (See *PROM* and *ROM*.)

E field   1. An electric field. 2. The electric field component of an electromagnetic wave.

electrically erasable PROM   A PROM that can be erased by an elec-

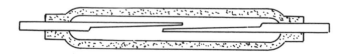

Figure A–8.   Dry-reed switch.

trical signal rather than by exposure to ultraviolet light. (Also see *PROM* and *ROM*.)

electrode   A body, point, or terminal in a device or circuit, which delivers electricity or to which electricity is applied. A positive electrode is an anode; a negative electrode, a cathode.

electromagnetic   Pertaining to the combined electric and magnetic fields associated with movements of electrons through conductors.

electromagnetic interference (EMI)   Disturbances of equipment operation caused by electromagnetic fields from outside sources in the atmosphere (for example, lightning or sunspots) or in the immediate vicinity (for example, power lines or electric motors).

electromotive force (EMF)   Pressure or voltage. The force which causes current to flow in a circuit.

electron   The subatomic particle that carries a negative charge of electricity. The electron has a mass of 9.109534×10^{-31} kilogram and carries a charge of 1.602189×10^{-19} coulomb.

electron drift   The movement of an electron from atom to atom in a conductor, as caused by the influence of an applied voltage.

electronic switch   A nonmechanical device, such as a flip-flop or gate, whose characteristic on-off operation can be used to make or break an electronic circuit. (Compare *contact switch*.)

EMF   Electromotive force.

EMI   Electromagnetic interference.

enclosure   A cabinet, case, or other housing for electronic equipment, such as a receiver, transmitter, or test instrument.

end-of-line resistor (E-O-L or EOL)   Resistance placed in a supervised detection circuit, usually at the farthest point from the alarm control unit, restricting the flow of current to a known value which is monitored. Shorting the circuit in an attempt to bypass sensors creates an increased flow of current, and causes an alarm. Opening (breaking) the circuit also triggers an alarm if the system is armed or a supervisory signal if the system is disarmed.

EPROM   Electrically programmable read-only memory.

F   1. Force. 2. Fluorine. 3. Fahrenheit. 4. Farad. 5. Focal length. 6. Symbol (on drawings) for filament; fuse. 7. Faraday constant.

Fahrenheit scale   A temperature scale on which the freezing point of water is 32 degrees, and the boiling point is 212 degrees. (Compare *Celsius scale*.)

farad (F)   The basic unit of capacitance. A capacitor has a capacitance of 1F when a change of 1 volt per second across the capacitor produces a current of 1 ampere through it. Named for Michael Faraday, 1791–1867.

fault   1. A defective point or region in a circuit or device. 2. A failure in a circuit or device.

ferrite bead   1. A magnetic storage device in the form of a bead of ferrite powder fused onto the signal conductors of a memory matrix. 2. A tiny bead that may be slipped over certain current carrying leads to choke out radio frequencies (see Figure A–9).

FET   Field-effect transistor.

fiber optics   1. Extruded materials, such as certain plastic filaments, which provide paths for light. 2. The art and science of developing and using such devices.

field test   A test of equipment under actual operating conditions, that is, outside the laboratory or factory.

fish   To push or pull a stiff steel wire or tape through a conduit or hollow cavity.

fixed contact   The stationary contact in a relay or switch. (Compare *movable contact.*)

flowchart   1. A diagram depicting the logic steps in a digital computer program. 2. A diagram showing the flow of material through a sequence of processes.

form A contact   Single-pole single-throw, normally open contact or relay.

form B contact   Single-pole single-throw, normally closed contact or relay.

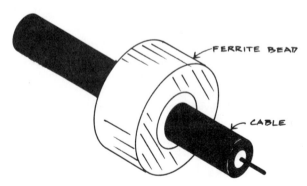

Figure A–9.   Ferrite bead.

form C contact   Single-pole double-throw contact or relay providing both normally open and normally closed outputs.

fortuitous conductor   A medium that creates an unwanted electrical path.

frequency   Symbol. f. The rate at which a phenomenon is repeated. The basic unit of frequency is the hertz (Hz), which is 1 cycle per second. Refers to the number of cycles per second of an alternating current (AC) or a radio frequency (RF) signal.

frequency-shift keying (FSK)   Keying a transmitter for telegraph or teletype communications (radio or wire) by shifting the carrier-frequency over a range of a few hundred hertz.

FSK   Frequency-shift keying.

gang   To mechanically couple components (pots, switches, etc.) for operation by a single knob.

gauge   1. A meter. 2. Wire data and measurements (see *American wire gauge*). 3. Sheet metal thickness (for example, 10 gauge).

Gel-cell battery   Trade name of Globe Union Inc. for a gelled electrolyte battery that can be recharged.

general-purpose relay   Any relay that can be used in various situations, such as for switching alternating or direct currents.

GFI   Ground-fault interrupter.

GHz   Gigahertz.

giga (G)   A prefix meaning billion, 10^9.

gigahertz (GHz)   A unit of high frequency; 1 GHz equals 1 billion cycles per second (1 billion Hz).

gigaohm   Symbol, GΩ. One billion ohms.

gnd   Ground.

grommet   An elastic washer inserted through a hole in a chassis or equipment enclosure to prevent accidental grounding of a conductor or to reduce wear on the cord or cable exiting the chassis.

ground   1. The earth in relation to electricity and magnetism. 2. An electrical connection to the ground. 3. The return point (usually negative) in a circuit. (Also see *ground connection*.) 4. A short circuit to the earth or to a circuit return point. 5. A short circuit to the metal chassis, case, or panel of a piece of equipment.

ground, chassis   A ground connection made to the metal chassis on a piece of equipment. When several ground connections are made to a single point on the chassis, a common ground results.

ground clamp   A device that provides a mechanical and electrical bond between a conductor and a ground rod or pipe. Generally capable of passing a large amount of current.

ground, cold water pipe Connection to a cold water pipe, which may run long distances under ground, helps ensure an effective electrical ground.

ground, common A single ground-point connection shared by several portions of a circuit or several devices.

ground connection A low resistance connection to the earth.

ground, direct A ground connection made by the shortest practicable route. (Compare *ground, indirect.*)

ground, earth 1. The portion of a circuit connected to a buried metallic object, like a grounding rod or water pipe. 2. A common connection to an electrode buried in the earth, such that good conductivity is maintained between the common circuit point and the earth itself. 3. A rod driven into the surface of the earth for use as a common circuit connection.

ground fault 1. Loss of a ground connection. 2. A short circuit to ground.

ground-fault interrupter (**GFI**) A fast-acting electronic circuit breaker that disconnects equipment from the power line to prevent electric shock or other damage when the safety ground connection is broken.

ground, indirect An unintentional ground connection (for example, accidental grounding of part of a circuit) or one obtained through a roundabout path. (Compare *ground, direct.*)

ground loop When two or more grounded points in an electrical system develop a conductive path between them rendering all or part of the detection circuit ineffective.

ground, negative In a direct-current power system, the connection of the negative pole to common ground.

ground, positive A direct-current electrical system in which the positive power supply terminal is connected to the common ground. Not generally used in the United States.

ground, true Actual ground, that is, the earth, as opposed to artificial ground, such as that provided by the radials of a ground-plane antenna or an equipment chassis.

ground rod A strong metal rod driven deep into the earth as a point of ground connection.

ground wire A conductor between an electrical or electronic device and a ground connection, either for circuit completion or for safety.

hair wire   1. An extremely thin wire filament in a lamp or bolometer. 2. Very small gauge wire (for example, No. 44).

half-cycle   Half of a complete AC alternation, that is, 180 degrees.

hand capacitance   Body capacitance, as evidenced between an operator's hand and sensitive circuit, for example.

hardwire   1. To construct a circuit for direct-current conductivity. 2. A circuit exhibiting direct-current conductivity over a complete, closed path. 3. To connect two or more alarm sensors or components with wire.

harness   A tied bundle of wires or cables for wiring electronic equipment.

heat-shrink tubing   An insulated flexible sleeving made from a plastic that shrinks permanently for a tight fit when heated; it is commonly used at the joint between a cable and connector.

Hertz (Hz)   A term replacing cycles-per-second as a unit of frequency. A unit of frequency equal to one cycle per second used in measuring radio waves and alternating current. Normal house current in the United States is 60Hz. Measurement is independent of voltage, current, or field strength.

HF   High frequency.

high frequency (HF)   Pertaining to frequencies in the 3 to 30 MHz band (wavelengths from 10 to 100 meters).

highway   An electrical bus or major circuit pathway.

homerun   A wiring method that connects individual sensors directly to the control panel instead of several sensors on a continuous circuit.

hookup   See *schematic diagram*.

hookup wire   Flexible wire (usually insulated) in electronic circuits.

Hz   Hertz.

I   Current.

IC   1. Integrated circuit. 2. Internal connection.

impedance   Symbol, Z. Unit, ohm. The combined resistance and reactance in an AC circuit. The total opposition that a circuit offers to the flow of alternating current or any other varying current at a particular frequency. It is a combination of resistance R and reactance X, measured in ohms.

indicating lamp   A lamp that is marked or coded so that when it is on or off it conveys information. For example, an illuminated lamp may show that power is on.

induced AC   A condition caused when low voltage wiring is placed near high voltage wiring. The higher voltage line may interfere with the lower voltage line and may interfere with or damage microprocessor-based equipment.

induced current   An alternating current established in one circuit by the alternating magnetic field of another circuit.

induced voltage   An AC voltage set up across one circuit (especially a coil) by the alternating magnetic field of another circuit.

inductance   Symbol, L. Unit, henry. In a conductor, device, or circuit, the inertial property (caused by an induced reverse voltage) that opposes the flow of current when a voltage is applied; it opposes a change in current that has been established.

infinity   Symbol, ∞. An infinite quantity, that is, one unlimited in duration or dimension. Thus, a quantity which may be increased or subdivided without limit is said to approach infinity.

infrared (**IR**)   Pertaining to the invisible rays (radiant energy) whose frequencies are just lower than those of visible red light. The infrared spectrum extends from approximately 1 to 4.3×10^2 THz (see Figure A−10).

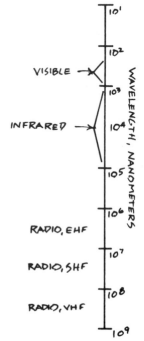

Figure A−10.   Infrared scale.

input   1. Energy or information delivered or transferred to a circuit or device. 2. The terminals of a device or circuit to which energy or information is applied. 3. To deliver or transfer energy or information to a circuit or device (as to input data from a computer peripheral to memory).

input voltage   Symbol, E_i or V_i. The voltage presented to a circuit or device. Compare output voltage.

insulating block   Blocks or pads used to separate safes and other metallic objects protected by capacitance detectors from ground.

insulation   A material having high resistance to the flow of electric current.

insulator   1. A material that, ideally, conducts no electricity; it can therefore be used for isolation and protection of energized circuits and components. 2. Any body made from an insulating material.

integrated circuit (IC)   A microminiature circuit usually mounted in a DIP plug or printed circuit board.

interference   The disturbing effect of any undesired signal.

international System of Units   Abbreviated SI (for *System International d'Unites*). International unit measurement system established in 1960 under the Treaty of the Meter.

ion   A charged atom, that is, one that either has gained one or more electrons (a negative ion, or anion) or lost one or more electrons (a positive ion, or cation).

IR   1. The product of current and resistance ($I \times R$). 2. Infrared.

jack   A receptacle for a plug. A plug (a male connector) is inserted into a jack (a female connector) to complete a circuit, or removed from it to break a circuit.

jacket   Pertaining to wire and cable, the outer sheath which protects wires against the environment and also may provide additional insulation.

jump   To provide a temporary circuit around a component or other circuit.

jump out   To bypass one or more sensors in a protective circuit.

jumper   A short piece of wire (usually flexible, insulated, and equipped with clips) for jumping a component or circuit. (See *jump*.)

junction   A joint (connection) between two conductors.

junction box   A (usually metal) protective box or can into which several conductors are brought together and connected.

K   1. Constant. 2. Dielectric constant. 3. Kelvin. 4. Computer memory storage capacity of 1024 bits. 5. Kilohm.

k Kilo.

kA Kiloampere.

kHz Kilohertz.

kilo (k) A prefix meaning thousand.

kilohertz (kHz) A unit of high frequency; 1kHz equals 10^3 cycles per second (1,000Hz).

lamp cord A two-wire insulated cord, used with low wattage appliances at 120 volts. The wire usually is 16- or 18-gauge (AWG) stranded copper.

latching relay An electromechanical or electronic relay that locks into the mode (on or off) into which it is energized.

Law of Averages In probability and statistics, the law stating that for a large sampling of events, the numerical probability value will be more closely approached than when the sampling is small. (Compare *Law of Large Numbers*.)

Law of Charges Unlike charges attract and like charges repel each other.

Law of Large Numbers In probability and statistics, the law stating that with a large sample, the sample average is extremely likely to approximate the population average. Often erroneously called *Law of Averages*.

Law of Magnetism Unlike magnetic poles attract and like magnetic poles repel each other.

Law of Reflection The angle of reflection is equal to the angle of incidence.

LCD Liquid-crystal display.

lead A conductor (usually a wire) leading to or emerging from a terminal or electrode.

lead-acid battery A storage battery in which the cells contain lead plates immersed in an electrolyte (like sulfuric acid). The positive plate contains lead peroxide, and the negative plate, spongy lead.

lead sulfate Formula, $PbSO_4$. An insulating compound formed in a lead-acid cell by the chemical action between the lead in the plates and the sulfuric acid electrolyte. If the sulfate is not broken down during charging of the cell, it eventually will ruin the cell.

lead sulfide Formula, PbS. A compound of lead and sulfer used as the light-sensitive material in some photoconductive cells.

lead zirconate titanate A synthetic piezoelectric material.

LED Light-emitting diode.

light-emitting diode (LED)   A diode, a solid-state device, which gives off virtually heatless colored light when electric current is passed through it. Very efficient and long-lasting. Common colors include red, green, and amber. Often used for digital readouts and annunciators.

lightning   The discharge that occurs between positive and negative poles in a thunderstorm. Generally, the negative pole is in the cloud and the positive pole is at the surface of the earth, resulting in a flow of electrons from cloud to ground. Some lightning occurs as a flow of electrons from ground to cloud, or between two clouds. These discharges may attain current levels of more than 100,000 amperes.

lightning arrester   A device that automatically bypasses to earth a heavy nearby lightning charge, thus protecting electronic equipment connected to an outdoor antenna or line.

line carrier   See *AC line carrier.*

line drop   The voltage drop along a line supplying power to a device.

line fault   A discontinuity in a transmission line, resulting in signal loss at the receiving end of a circuit.

liquid-crystal display (LCD)   For counters, calculators, digital meters, and digital clocks, a readout device in which each digit is formed by stripes of liquid-crystal material.

lithium   Symbol, Li. An element of the alkali-metal group. Atomic number, 3. Atomic weight, 6.940. Lithium is the lightest metal known.

lithium cell   A vented, steel-jacketed primary cell in which the anode element is lithium. The electrolyte is an organic substance without water. Nominal voltage is 2.8 V. Lithium cells usually have long shelf lives.

load   1. A device or circuit that is operated by the energy output of another device or circuit. 2. The power output capability of a power-producing device.

loop   A signal path (for example, a feedback loop). A term commonly used for an alarm system's detection circuit. A closed circuit with detection devices connected in series. Through common usage, "loop" also refers to any detection loop, whether normally closed or normally open.

loop resistance   The total resistance of two conductors measured round trip from one end.

loss   A reduction in signal level or strength. Usually expressed in decibels.

M   1. Mega. 2. Roman numeral for 10^3.

m   1. Meter. 2. Mile (also, mi).

mA   Milliampere.

macro   Prefix denoting extremely large. (Compare *micro.*)

magnet   A device or body of material which has the ability to attract to itself pieces of iron and other magnetic metals, and the ability to attract or repel other magnets.

magnet charger   A device that produces an intense magnetic field for restoring weakened magnets or for making new magnets.

main   British variation of domestic AC power supply.

mains   In a power distribution center, the lines that supply the entire system. An example is the set of mains leading into a house.

make   1. The closing of contacts. 2. To close contacts.

man-made interference   Electrical interference generated by circuits, devices, and machines, as opposed to *natural interference.*

manual   1. Actuated or operated directly by mechanical means rather than automatically. 2. The book or booklet that describes the operation and maintenance of an electronic device.

mean   A simple average of two or more numbers.

mechanical joint   A union of electrical conductors consisting exclusively of a junction or splice made without brazing, soldering, or welding.

mechanical switch   A switch in which the contacts are opened or closed by means of a depressable plunger or other physical (mechanical) action.

meg   Megohm (also, M).

mega (M)   A prefix meaning million, 10^6.

megahertz (MHz)   A unit of high frequency, 1 million cycles per second. $1MHz = 10^6 Hz$.

megampere (MA)   A unit of high current; $1MA = 10^6$ amperes.

megavolt (MV)   A unit of high voltage; $1MV = 10^6$ volts.

megavolt-ampere (MVA)   A unit of high reactive power. $1MVA = 10^6$ volt-amperes.

megawatt (MW)   A unit of high power. $1MW = 10^6$ watts.

megohm   Symbol, $M\Omega$. A unit of high resistance, reactance, or impedance. $1M\Omega = 10^6$ ohms.

megohmmeter   A special ohmmeter for measuring resistances in the megohm range.

mercury switch   A switch consisting essentially of two or more stiff wire electrodes and a drop of mercury hermetically sealed in a glass tube. Tilting the tube causes the mercury to flow toward one end where it immerses the electrodes, providing a conductive path between them.

metallic circuit   A circuit, such as a two-wire telephone line, in which earth ground is not a part of the circuit.

metal-oxide silicon field-effect transistor (MOSFET)   A field-effect transistor in which the gate electrode is not a pn junction (as in the junction field-effect transistor) but a thin metal film insulated from the semiconductor channel by a thin oxide film. Gate control action, therefore, is entirely electrostatic. Drain and source electrodes are pn junctions. Also called insulated-gate field-effect transistor.

metal-oxide varistor (MOV)   A varistor in which the resistance material is a metallic oxide such as zinc oxide.

meter   1. An instrument for measuring and indicating the value of a particular quantity. (See, for example, *voltmeter*.) 2. A metric unit of linear measure (abbreviated m). 1m = 39.37 inches.

mF   Millifarad.

MHz   Megahertz.

mi   Mile (also, m).

micro   1. A prefix meaning millionth, that is, 10^{-6} Symbol, μ. 2. A prefix meaning extremely small (as in microstructure). (Compare *macro*.)

microammeter   A usually direct reading instrument employed to measure current in the microampere range. (Also see *current meter*.)

microampere (μA)   A small unit of current. $1\mu A = 10^{-6}$ amperes.

microcircuit   An extremely small circuit fabricated upon and within a substrate such as a semiconductor chip. (Also see *integrated circuit*.)

microfarad (μF)   A unit of low capacitance. $1\mu F = 10^{-6}$ farads.

microhm   Symbol, $\mu\Omega$. A unit of low resistance, reactance, or impedance, $1\mu\Omega = 10^{-6}$.

microhmmeter   An instrument for measuring ultralow resistance. Such an instrument must have a special provision for cancelling the effects of contact and lead resistance.

microminiature   Pertaining to an extremely small body, component, or circuit; the last adjective in the sequence *standard, small, midget, miniature, subminature, microminature*.

microsecond   Symbol, μs. A small unit of time equal to 1 millionth of a second. $1\mu s = 10^{-6}$ seconds.

microvolt   Symbol, μV. A unit of low voltage. 1μV $= 10^{-6}$ volts.

microvoltmeter   A usually direct reading instrument employed to measure voltages in the microvolt range. An input amplifier boosts the test voltage sufficiently to deflect the indicating meter.

microwatt   Symbol, μW. A unit of low power, especially electrical power. 1μW $= 10^{-6}$ watts.

microwattmeter   An instrument for measuring power in the microwatt range. Such an instrument obtains its sensitivity from a built-in input amplifier.

midget   Of reduced size (smaller than small and larger than miniature).

mil   A small unit of linear measure. 1 mil $= 10^{-3}$ inch $= 0.0254$ mm.

milli (m)   A prefix meaning thousandth, that is, 10^{-3}.

milliammeter   A usually direct reading instrument for measuring current in the milliampere range.

milliampere (mA)   A unit of low current; 1mA $= 10^{-3}$ ampere.

milliampere-hour (mAH)   A unit of low current drain or charging rate. 1mAH $= 10^{-3}$ ampere-hour. (Also see *ampere-hour* and *battery capacity*.)

millifarad (mF)   A small unit of capacitance. 1mF $= 10^{-3}$ farad. (Also see *farad*.)

milligram (mg)   A metric unit of weight equal to 10^{-3} gram.

milliohm   Symbol, mΩ. A small unit of resistance, reactance, or impedance. 1m$\Omega = 10^{-3}$.

milliohmmeter   An ohmmeter for measuring resistances in the milliohm range.

millisecond (ms)   A small unit of time. 1ms $= 10^{-3}$ second.

millivolt (mV)   A unit of low voltage. 1mV $= 10^{-3}$ volts. (Also see *volt*.)

millivoltmeter   A usually direct reading instrument for measuring electric potential. Its sensitivity is provided by a high-gain amplifier operated ahead of the indicating meter.

milliwatt (mW)   A small unit of electric power; 1 mW $= 10^{-3}$ watt. (Also see *watt* and *microwatt*.)

milliwattmeter   An instrument for measuring power in milliwatts. Such instruments usually obtain their sensitivity from a built-in preamplifier.

miniature   Very small (smaller than *midget* and larger than *subminiature*).

mode   Operational condition.

module   An assembly containing a complete self-contained circuit (or subcircuit) and often miniaturized and made for plug-in operation. A self-contained unit or component.

momentary-contact switch   A switch that maintains contact only while it is held down. Such a switch may be a pushbutton device, a toggle switch, a slide-switch, or a lever switch.

MOSFET   Metal-oxide silicon field-effect transistor.

motherboard   In a computer or data processing device, the circuit board on which most of the main circuitry is mounted.

MOV   Metal-oxide varistor.

movable contact   The traveling contact in a relay or switch. (Compare *fixed contact.*)

mu   1. Micro, that is, a typewritten substitute for the Greek letter μ. 2. The 12th letter (M, μ) of the Greek alphabet. 3. The symbol (μ) for amplification factor, permeability, the prefix micro, micron, electrical moment, inductivity, magnetic moment, and molecular conductivity.

multiconductor cable   A cable consisting of two or more conductors, either cabled or laid in a flat parallel construction with or without a common overall covering.

multicontact switch   A switch having more than two contacting positions.

multimeter   A meter that allows measurement of different quantities (for example, current, voltage, and resistance); the functions are usually made available through a selector switch.

multiposition switch   A switch having more than two contacting positions.

multitester   An instrument such as a multimeter or a combined signal generator and oscilloscope, that performs a number of different test functions.

MV   Megavolt.

mV   Millivolt.

MVA   Megavolt-ampere.

MW   Megawatt.

μ   1. Micro. 2. Micron. 3. Permeability. 4. Inductivity. 5. Molecular conductance. 6. Electric moment. 7. Magnetic moment. 8. Coefficient of friction. 9. Amplification factor.

μA   Microampere.

μF   Microfarad.

μΩ   Microhm (also, *μ*ohm).

μV   Microvolt.

n   1. Nano.

nano (n)   A prefix meaning billionth, that is, 10^{-9}.

National Electric Code (NEC)   Safety regulations and procedures issued by the National Fire Protection Association for the installation of electric wiring and equipment in the United States. Although the code is advisory from the Association's standpoint, it is enforced to various degrees by local authorities.

natural interference   Interference from atmospheric electricity—the sun, stars, etc.—as opposed to *man-made interference.*

NC   1. Normally closed. (See *circuit, closed.*) 2. On drawings, abbreviation of no connection.

NEC   National Electric Code.

neg   Negative.

negative   1. Possessing negative electrification. 2. Opposite of positive. 3. In numbers, less than zero.

negative charge   An electric charge consisting of a quantity of negative electrification. (Compare *positive charge.*)

negative conductor   The conductor or wire connected to the negative terminal of a current, power, or voltage source.

negative number   A number less than zero, that is, one to which the minus sign (−) is assigned.

nickel-cadmium battery   1. A battery of nickel-cadmium cells. 2. Loosely, a nickel-cadmium cell.

nickel-cadmium cell   A small 1.2V rechargeable cell in which the anode is cadmium; the cathode, nickel hydroxide; and the electrolyte, potassium hydroxide.

NO   Normally open. (See *circuit, open.*)

no-load current   1. Output-electrode current (for example, plate or collector current) when a device is not delivering output to an external load. 2. Current flowing in the primary winding of an unloaded transformer.

no-load voltage   The open-circuit output voltage of a power supply, amplifier, generator, or network.

nominal   Approximate, and specified as a typical example only, for the purpose of identifying the operating or value range. For example, a power supply circuit may have a nominal rating of 12V even though it may be operated within a range of 11 to 13.8V.

nominal current   The rated value of required current or of current output. (Also see *nominal value.*)

nominal resistance   The rated value of resistance of a resistor or similar device. (Also see *nominal value.*)

nominal value   The labeled value specified without reference to tolerance. The nominal value may differ significantly from the true value.

nominal voltage   The rated value of required voltage or of voltage output. (Also see *nominal value.*)

nonchargeable battery   A primary battery, that is, one that cannot ordinarily be recharged.

nonpolar   1. Having no pole(s). 2. Pertaining to atoms which share electrons to complete their outer shells. 3. Not polarized nor requiring polarization.

nonpolarized electrolytic capacitor   An electrolytic capacitor which has no definite negative and positive terminals and, consequently, can be operated on AC circuits.

nonshorting switch   A multiple-throw switch that disconnects one circuit before completing another; that is, no two poles are ever connected simultaneously.

normally closed (NC)   The condition of a switch or relay whose contacts are closed when the device is at rest. (Compare *normally open.*)

normally open (NO)   The condition of a switch or relay whose contacts are open when the device is at rest. (Compare *normally closed.*)

nucleus   The center or core of an atom. The nucleus contains electrons, neutrons, protons, and other particles. The net electric charge of the nucleus is positive, and is equal to the sum of the negative charges of the orbital electrons of the atom.

null point   In a balanced circuit such as a bridge or potentiometer, the point of zero output voltage (or current) or minimum output voltage (or current).

numerator   The term above the bar in a fraction; the number being divided. (Compare *denominator.*)

OD   Outside diameter.

ohm   Symbol, Ω. Unit of resistance such that a constant current of one ampere produces a force of one volt. (See also *resistance.*)

Ohm's Law   The basis of all electric circuits which establishes the relationship between voltage, current, and resistance. In DC circuits, current is directly proportional to voltage, and inversely proportional to resistance. The law is expressed in the formula $I = E/R$, where I equals current (amperes), E equals voltage (volts) and R equals resistance (ohms). For AC circuits, Ohm's law shows that $I = E/X = E/Z$, where X is reactance, and Z is impedance. (Indispensable information for designing—or defeating—a security system.)

ohmic value   Electrical resistance expressed in ohms or multiples or fractions thereof.

ohmmeter   An instrument for the direct measurement of electrical resistance.

ohmmeter zero   1. The condition of proper adjustment of an ohmmeter, indicating zero resistance for a direct short circuit. 2. The potentiometer, or other control, used for adjusting an ohmmeter to obtain a reading of zero with a short circuit.

omega   The last letter of the Greek alphabet. Capital omega, Ω, is the symbol for ohm.

open circuit   See *circuit, open.*

optimum voltage   The value of voltage which results in the most effective performance of a circuit or device.

oscilloscope   An instrument that presents for visual inspection the pattern representing variations in an electrical quantity.

outage   1. Loss of power to a system. 2. Loss of a received signal.

outlet   A male or female receptacle which delivers a signal or operating power to equipment plugged into it.

output   1. Energy or information delivered by a circuit, device, or system. (Compare *input.*) 2. The terminals at which energy or information is taken from a circuit, device, or system.

output voltage   Symbol, E_o. 1. The voltage delivered by a source, such as a battery, generator, or amplifier. (Compare *input voltage.*) 2. The voltage across the output leg or electrode of a circuit or device.

overload   1. Drain in excess of the rated output of a circuit or device. 2. An excessive driving signal.

override   1. To go around an automatic control system intentionally. 2. To bridge a functional stage of a system.

p   Pico.

paddle-handle switch   A toggle switch, the lever of which is a flattened rod (see Figure A–11). Compare bat-handle switch, rocker switch, and slide switch.

pair   1. Two wires, especially two insulated conductors in a cable. 2. A couple of particles.

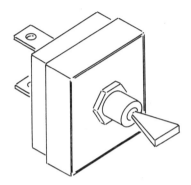

Figure A–11.   Paddle-handle switch.

paired cable   A cable made up of separate twisted pairs of conducting wires.

panel   A plate on which are mounted the controls and indicators of an equipment, for easy access to the operator.

parallel   The condition in which two comparably sized objects or figures are equidistant at all facing points.

parallel circuit   A circuit in which the components are connected across each other, that is, so that the circuit segment could be drawn showing component leads bridging common conductors as rungs would across a ladder. Circuit interconnection in which all components share a common positive and common negative connection. Normally open devices are connected in parallel circuits. Compare series circuit.

parallel-series circuit   A circuit consisting of parallel circuits connected in series with each other. (Also see *parallel circuit* and *series circuit.*)

patch   1. A temporary connection, as between a radio receiver and a telephone or, conversely, between a telephone line and a radio transmitter. 2. To make quick, usually temporary connections, as with a patch cord.

patch cord   A flexible line of one or more conductors with a jack or connector at each end, used to interconnect (patch) circuit points exposed for the purpose on a panel or breadboard.

path   1. The route over which current flows. 2. In radio and navigation, the imaginary line extending directly between transmitter and receiver (or target). 3. In a computer program, the logical order of instructions.

PC   Printed circuit.

PCB   Printed-circuit board.

PC board   See *printed-circuit board.*

percent (%)   An expression of a fraction, in terms of hundredths. A quantity of x percent indicates a fraction of $x/100$.

pico (p)   1. A prefix meaning trillionth, that is, 10^{-12}. 2. A prefix meaning very small.

pictorial wiring diagram   A wiring diagram in the form of a drawing or photograph of the components, as opposed to one of symbols. The components are shown in their positions in the finished equipment, and the wiring as lines running between them.

piezo   A prefix meaning pressure.

piezoelectric ceramic   A ceramic which delivers a voltage when deformed; or conversely, which changes in shape when voltage is applied to it.

piezoelectric crystal   A crystal, such as quartz, tourmaline, or various synthetics, that delivers a voltage when mechanical force is applied between its faces, or which changes its shape when an electromotive force is applied between its faces.

pigtail   1. A usually long and sometimes flexible lead, such as the pigtail of a fixed capacitor. 2. Descriptive of a device containing a long lead or leads, and usually mounted by such leads.

plenum   The air return path of a central air handling system, either ductwork or open space over a dropped ceiling.

plenum cable   Cable approved by Underwriters Laboratories for installation in plenums without the need for conduit.

plug   A type of quick-connect device (usually male) which is inserted into a jack to make a circuit connection, or pulled out of the jack to break the connection.

polarity   The condition of being positive or negative (electricity), or north or south (magnetism). The direction of electron flow, from negative to positive, in direct-current circuits.

polarized capacitor   A conventional electrolytic capacitor; so called because one particular terminal of this capacitor must be connected to the most positive terminal of the two connection points. (Compare *nonpolarized electrolytic capacitor.*)

polyvinyl chloride (PVC)   A plastic insulating material. Dielectric constant, 3.6 to 4.0. Dielectric strength, 800V/mil.

positive   1. Possessing a positive polarity. 2. Opposite of negative. 3. Greater than zero.

positive charge   An electrical charge characterized by having fewer electrons than a negative charge. (Compare *negative charge.*)

positive conductor   The conductor or line connected to the positive terminal of a current, voltage, or power source. (Compare *negative conductor.*)

pot   1. Potentiometer. 2. Dashpot. 3. Potential. 4. To encapsulate a circuit in a potting compound, such as epoxy resin.

potentiometer   1. A variable resistor employed as a voltage divider. The input voltage is applied to the ends of the resistance element, and the output is taken from the slider (wiper) and one end of the element.

potted circuit   A circuit which is potted in a suitable plastic or wax.

potted component   An electronic pat which is potted in a suitable plastic or wax.

potting   Embedding a component or circuit in a solid mass of plastic or wax held in a container. The process is similar to encapsulation, except that in potting, the container (envelope) remains part of the assembly. (In encapsulation, the mold is removed after the encapsulating material has dried and hardened.)

power consumption   1. For a direct-current device, the normal operating voltage multiplied by the normal drawn current. 2. For an alternating-current circuit, the root-mean-square voltage multiplied by the root-mean-square current.

power drain   The amount of power drawn by a device. It may be operating power or standby power.

power loss   Power that is dissipated in a component; this power generates heat while doing no useful work and therefore represents energy loss—except when the generation of heat is the end purpose.

power rating   1. The specified power required by a device for normal operation. 2. The specified power output of a generator or amplifier.

power supply   A device, such as a generator or a transformer-rectifier-filter arrangement, that produces the power needed to operate an electronic device.

printed circuit (PC)   A pattern of conductors (corresponding to the wiring of an electronic circuit) formed on a board of insulating material.

printed-circuit board (PCB)   A usually copperclad plastic board used to make a printed circuit.

probe   A usually slender pencil-like implement with a pointed metal tip and flexible, insulated lead, used to make contact with live points in a circuit under test (for example, voltmeter probe, oscilloscope probe).

programmable read-only memory (PROM)   In a computer or computer-based device, a ROM that can store a program by use of PROM programmer.

PROM   Programmable read-only memory.

PROM programmer   An electronic device which, through the use of a built-in keyboard, can be made to store a program in a PROM.

pull switch   A mechanical switch actuated by a pulling action.

PVC   Polyvinyl chloride.

QMQB   Quick make, quick break.

quad   1. A combination of four components—such as diodes, transistors, etc.—in a single housing. The components usually are carefully matched. 2. In a cable, a combination of four separately insulated conductors (sometimes two twisted pairs) twisted together.

quasi   An adjective meaning to some extent or like, as in quasioptical wave (a radio wave that behaves like a light ray).

quick break   An operating characteristic of a switch, relay, or circuit breaker whereby the contacts open rapidly, even when the actuating current or mechanical force is slow acting.

quick-break switch   A switch that opens rapidly, although its handle or lever is moved slowly by the operator. This action minimizes arcing and prevents chatter. (Compare *quick-make switch.*)

quick-disconnect   The characteristic of a connector which enables its mating halves to be separated quickly and simply in order to break the circuit in which it is installed.

quick make   An operating characteristic of a switch, relay, or circuit breaker whereby the contacts close rapidly, even when the actuating current or mechanical force is slow acting.

quick-make switch   A switch that closes rapidly, although its handle or lever is moved slowly by the operator. (*Compare quick-break switch.*)

R   Resistance (in Ohm's law).

raceway   A protective shield installed over surface wiring for safety and physical protection of the wires. (See also *wire duct* and *wireways.*)

rack   An upright frame for holding equipment of rack-and-panel construction.

radiant energy   All forms of energy emitted by a source and moving like a wave through space. Included are radio waves, light, heat, x-rays, radioactive emissions, and other types of energy. Sound waves are often included, but sound requires air or some other form of matter for its transmission.

radiation   1. The emission of energy or particles (for example, waves from an antenna, x-rays from an x-ray tube, energy from radioactive material, heat from a body). 2. Narrowly, x-rays and the emissions from radioactive substances. 3. The emission (1 or 2, above) itself.

radio frequency (**RF**)   The frequency of certain electromagnetic waves. This term usually is applied to "wireless" alarm systems which use radio frequencies to transmit alarm and supervisory signals from detectors with transmitters to a receiver and control panel.

radio-frequency interference (**RFI**)   Electromagnetic interference in the radio frequency range. Radio frequencies, imposed accidentally or deliberately on a radio-frequency signal which degrade or destroy the ability to transmit or receive proper signal information.

radio spectrum   The continuum of frequencies useful for radio communication and control. These frequencies have been classified in the following manner: very low frequencies (VLF), 10 to 30kHz; low frequencies (LF), 30 to 300kHz; medium frequencies (MF), 300 to 3,000kHz; high frequencies (HF), 3 to 30MHz; very high frequencies (VHF), 30 to 3,000MHz; ultrahigh frequencies (UHF), 300 to 3,000MHz; superhigh frequencies (SHF), 3 to 30GHz.

RAM   Random-access memory.

random-access memory   In computer and data processing systems, a memory providing access time that is independent of the address.

range   1. The limits within which a circuit or device operates, that is, the territory defined by such limits (for examples, current range, frequency range, voltage range). 2. The difference between the upper and lower limits of deflection of a meter. 3. The distance over which a transmitter operates reliably. 4. The area covered by a space protection device.

raw AC   Unrectified alternating current or voltage.

reactance   Symbol, X. Unit, ohm. The opposition offered to the flow of alternating current by pure capacitance, pure inductance, or a combination of the two. Reactance introduces phase shift. (Compare *resistance*.)

read-only memory (**ROM**)   In a computer or calculator, a memory unit in which instructions or data are permanently stored for use by the machine or for reference by the user. The stored information is read out nondestructively, and no information can subsequently be written into the memory.

redundancy   1. The repetition of components in a circuit (for example, series or parallel connection of them) so that one will be available for circuit operation if the other fails. 2. Having available more than one method for performing a function. 3. Having on hand several copies of data or pieces of equipment as a safeguard against loss or damage.

reed   A usually thin metal blade, leaf, or strip employed in vibrators, reed-type relays, reed-type switches, and similar devices.

reed switch   A type of magnetic contact switch with metallic reeds sealed in a glass tube.

regulated power supply   A power supply whose output is held automatically to a constant level or within a narrow range, regardless of loading variation.

relay   1. A signal-actuated switching device that opens and/or closes contacts when voltage is applied or removed. In most instances, a relatively weak current or voltage is used to make the relay switch a higher current or voltage. A relay may be electromechanical or fully electronic (no moving parts). 2. A radio signal repeater station.

resistance   Symbol, R. Unit, ohm. In a device, component, or circuit, the simple opposition to current flow. In Ohm's law, $R = E/I$, where E is voltage, and I is current. The electrical equivalent of friction. A measure of the difficulty of moving electrical current through a medium when voltage is applied. Resistance is measured in ohms.

resistance drop   The voltage drop across a resistor, or across the inherent resistance of a device.

resistive load   A load device which is essentially a pure resistance.

resistor   A device having resistance concentrated in lumped form. (Also see *resistance*.)

RFI   Radio-frequency interference.

RG/U   Military shorthand for certain types of coaxial cable.

rheostat   A variable dropping resistor usually of the rotary type but often of the long slider type.

ripple   A usually small AC voltage or current occurring in a DC component as an unavoidable byproduct of rectification of commutation.

rocker switch   A toggle switch, the lever of which is a specially shaped bar which is rocked back and forth to operate the switch. (Compare *bat-handle switch, paddle switch,* and *slide switch.*)

ROM   Read-only memory.

rosin   A resin derived chemically from an extract of pine wood and used in some solders.

rotary relay   An electromechanical relay in which a pivoted armature rotates to open or close the contacts.

rotary switch   A switch in which a blade moves in a circle or in arcs over the contacts.

route   1. To physically position wires or conducting circuit paths by planning and deliberation. 2. The path over which conductors are positioned. 3. A path over which signals or information may be carried.

schematic diagram   Circuit diagram. Also called wiring diagram and schematic.

selector switch   A multiposition switch (usually rotary).

semiconductor   A material whose resistivity lies between that of conductors and insulators (for example, germanium and silicon).

sensor   A device which samples a phenomenon (electrical or nonelectrical) and delivers a proportionate current or voltage in terms of which the phenomenon may be measured, or with which control action can be initiated.

sequenced relay   A relay whose several contacts close in a predetermined order.

series circuit   A circuit whose components are, in effect, connected in a string, or end to end, creating a single current path in a normally closed circuit. (Compare *parallel circuit.*)

service loop   A surplus of wire looped at one or more points in the wire run for future system modifications or servicing.

sheath   The outer covering or jacket of a multiconductor cable.

shelf life   The longest time electronic equipment may be stored before deterioration of materials or degradation of performance is evidenced.

shield   In cables, a metallic layer placed around a conductor or group of conductors to prevent electrostatic interference between the enclosed wires and external fields.

shield braid   Tubing woven from wire, through which an insulated wire is passed and thus shielded.

shielded cable   Cable completely enclosed within a metal sheath that is either flexible or rigid.

shielded wire   A single strand of insulated wire completely enclosed in a flexible or rigid shield.

shock   A sudden stimulation of nerves and convulsive contraction of muscles caused by a discharge of electricity through the body.

shunt   1. To bypass or remove devices from a circuit. 2. A short circuit or bypass for electric current in a circuit.

SI   International System of Units.

signal   An electrical quantity, such as current or voltage, that can be used to convey information for communication, control, calculation, and other uses.

single-pole, double-throw (SPDT)   Descriptive of an electrical, electronic, or mechanical switch with a pole that can be connected to either of two adjacent poles, but not to both.

single-pole, single-throw (SPST)   Descriptive of an electrical, electronic, or mechanical switch with a pole that can be connected to an adjacent pole (or disconnected from it) at will. It is used to provide the make and break function in a single circuit.

single-throw switch   A single-action switch with two or more poles.

slide switch   A switch which is actuated by sliding back and forth a blockshaped button. (Compare *bat-handle switch, paddle switch,* and *rocker switch.*)

slow-blow fuse   A fuse in which the melting wire breaks apart slowly. The time delay allows the fuse to withstand momentary surges which would not damage the protected equipment.

slow-break fast-make relay   A relay that opens slowly and closes rapidly.

slow-break slow-make relay   A relay that opens slowly and closes slowly.

slow-make fast-break relay   A relay that closes slowly and opens rapidly.

slow-make slow-break relay   A relay that closes slowly and opens slowly.

snake   1. A long, strong, flexible wire or strip used to pull other wires through pipes or tubes. 2. To route wires or cables through a group or circuits, components, or boards.

soft-drawn wire   Wire that is highly malleable, therefore easily bent and unbent.

solder   1. A metal alloy (usually of tin and lead) which is melted to join pieces of other metals. 2. To join metals with solder.

soldering   Joining (usually nonferrous) metal parts with solder, a lead-alloy substance.

soldering gun   An electric soldering iron having the general shape of a pistol. Also called solder gun and soldering pistol.

soldering iron   An electric or nonelectric tool having a heated tip for melting solder.

solderless connection   A connection between leads or leads and terminals, accomplished entirely through crimping, pinching, splicing, and the like. (See *mechanical connection*.)

solderless terminal   A terminal to which a solderless connection can be made.

solid conductor   A conductor consisting of a single drain wire.

solid wire   Wire consisting of a single strand of metal. (Compare *stranded wire*.)

SPDT   Single-pole, double-throw (switch or relay).

specification   1. A precise listing of needs. 2. For an electronic device, a statement of performance over specific parameters (for example, a specification for a passive infrared intrusion sensor might be to cover an area of a certain size and shape).

speed of light   The velocity of light in air or vacuum; in a vacuum, in which case the symbol is c, it is 300,000 kilometers per second (186,000 miles per second).

speed of sound   The velocity of sound depends on the transmission medium. At ordinary temperatures, sound travels approximately 344 meters (1,129 feet) per second in air and 1,463 meters (4,800 feet) per second in water.

speed of transmission   The amount of data sent in a given unit of time. Generally measured in bits per second, characters per second, characters per minute, or words per minute. Used primarily for digital codes.

spike   A momentary increase in electrical voltage or current. Spikes can damage electronic equipment.

splice   1. A joint of two wires made essentially by tightly winding their ends together for a short distance and sometimes soldering for additional strength and rigidity. 2. To make such a joint.

SPST   Single-pole, single-throw (switch or relay).

standby battery   An emergency power source in case the primary power source fails.

static electricity   Energy in the form of a stationary electric charge, such as that stored in capacitors and thunderclouds or produced by friction or induction.

status   The condition of a system, zone, circuit, or sensor at a particular time.

step-down transformer   A transformer delivering an output voltage that is lower than the input voltage. In such a transformer, the secondary (output) winding contains fewer turns than the primary (input) winding. (Compare *step-up transformer.*)

step-up transformer   A transformer delivering an output voltage that is higher than the input voltage. In such a transformer, the secondary (output) winding contains more turns than the primary (input) winding. (Compare *step-down transformer.*)

strand   A single wire.

stranded conductor   A conductor composed of solid wires twisted together, either singly or in groups.

stranded wire   A conductor composed of several wires twisted together into a kind of cable. (Compare *solid wire.*)

subminiature   A size designation between *miniature* and *microminiature.*

supply current   Alternating or direct current available for operating equipment.

supply power   The power of an AC or DC supply.

supply voltage   The voltage of an AC or DC supply.

sw   Switch.

switch   1. Abbreviated sw. A circuit or device (electronic, electromechanical, or mechanical) for opening and closing a circuit or for connecting a line to one of several different lines (for example, rotary selector switch). 2. To change the logic state of a circuit or device. 3. To cause an electrical circuit to change states, as from on to off or vice versa.

system   1. An integrated assemblage of elements operating together to accomplish a prescribed end purpose, for example, alarm system, servo system, communication system. The elements often are completely self-contained. 2. A methodology incorporating fixed and ordered procedures for accomplishing an end purpose.

T   1. Transformer. 2. Tetra. 3. Ton.

tensile strength   The pull stress required to break a given item. The term usually is applied to wire.

terminal   A connection point for circuit or other wires.

terminal block   A block with several terminals, intended for interconnection of circuits.

terminal board   An insulating board carrying several lugs, tabs, or screws as terminals.

terminal strip   A strip of insulating material, such as plastic or ceramic, on which are mounted one or more screws, lugs (see Figure A–12), or other terminals to create multiple connection points for wires.

test   A procedure consisting of one or several steps, in which (1) the mode of operation of a circuit or device is established, (2) the value of a component is ascertained, or (3) the behavior of a circuit or device is observed.

test lead   The flexible, insulated wire attached to a test prod.

test point   A terminal intended for connection of test equipment in the repair or debugging of a circuit. Often, test points are labeled by the letters TP followed by a numeral, such as TP1, TP2, and so on.

test prod   A stick-type probe with a flexible, insulated lead terminating in a plug or lug for attachment to an instrument.

tetra   Prefix meaning 1 trillion, 10^{12}.

tetrahertz (THz) $1 \text{THz} = 10^{12}$ hertz.

thermal shock   The effect of applying heat or cold to a device so rapidly that abnormal reactions occur, such as rapid (often catastrophic) expansions and contractions.

THz   Tetrahertz.

tie   A bracket, clamp, clip, ring, or strip for holding several wires tightly as a cable or bundle (see Figure A–13).

tie point   A lug, screw, or other terminal to which wires are connected at a junction.

tinned copper   Tin coating added to copper to aid in soldering and inhibit corrosion.

toggle   A bistable device.

toggle switch   A switch having a mechanism that snaps into the on or off position at the opposite extremes to which a lever is moved.

Figure A–12.   Terminal switch.

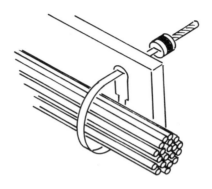

Figure A-13.   Tie.

tolerance   The amount by which error is allowed in a value, rating, dimension, and so on. It is usually expressed as a percent of nominal value, plus and minus so many units of measurement.

transformer   A device employing electromagnetic induction to transfer electrical energy from one circuit to another, that is, without direction connection between them. In its simplest form, a transformer consists of separate primary and secondary coils wound on a common core of ferromagnetic material, such as iron. When an alternating current flows through the primary coil, the resulting magnetic flux in the core induces an alternating voltage across the secondary coil; the induced voltage may cause a current to flow in an external circuit. (Also see *air-core transformer, induction, inductive coupling, iron-core transformer,* and *turns ratio.*)

transient   A brief power surge in an electrical line.

trouble condition   An abnormal system or circuit condition.

trouble signal   A signal resulting from a trouble condition.

troubleshoot   1. To look for the cause of equipment failure. 2. Debug.

TV   1. Television. 2. Terminal velocity.

twisted pair   A wire line, consisting of two separately insulated conductors twisted about each other, used for alarm system detection circuits communications.

UHF   Ultrahigh frequency.

UL or U.L.   Underwriters Laboratories.

ultra   A prefix meaning above or higher than (for example, ultraviolet, ultrahigh frequency, ultrasonics).

ultrahigh frequency   A radio frequency in the range 300 to 3,000MHz.

unbalanced cable   (Single-conductor, 75-ohm shielded coaxial cable, like RG-11/U and RG-59/U, commonly used in CCTV applications.

underground cable   A cable that is buried in the earth.

Underwriters Laboratories   A private corporation which issues standards of safety for components, equipment, and their operation. Many pieces of electronic equipment are labeled with the Underwriters Laboratories seal.

unloaded battery   1. A battery in the standby condition. 2. A battery tested for open-circuit terminal voltage, that is, with no load except the voltmeter.

unregulated   Not held to a constant value. For example, an unregulated voltage is free to fluctuate in value.

unregulated power supply   A power supply whose output current or voltage is not automatically held to a constant value.

V   Volt.

VA   Volt-ampere.

V/A   Volts per ampere (ohms).

VAC   Volts AC.

valence electrons   Electrons in the outermost orbits of an atom. It is these electrons which determine the chemical and physical properties of a material. (Also see *free electron*.)

variable resistor   A resistor whose value can be varied either continuously or in steps.

variable transformer   A transformer (often an autotransformer) whose output voltage is adjustable from zero (or some minimum value) to maximum. For this purpose, either the primary or the secondary is provided with a number of taps. But usually smooth variation is provided by a wiper arm that slides over the turns of one coil.

velocity of light   Symbol, c. The speed at which light moves through space, that is, through a vacuum. The velocity of light, an important figure in electronics, is 299,792 kilometers per second (186,282 miles per second).

velocity of radio waves   The speed at which radio waves move through space. This velocity is the same as that of light.

velocity of sound   The speed at which sound travels through a medium. This varies considerably for different media; through air it is approximately 344 m/s (1,129 feet per second), whereas through glass, at the same temperature, it is 5501.64 m/s (18,050 feet per second).

very high frequency (VHF)   Radio frequencies in the range 30 to 300MHz.

very low frequency (VLF)   A radio frequency in the range 10 to 30kHz.

VHF   Very high frequency.

V_i Input voltage.

VLF   Very low frequency.

V_o Output voltage.

VOA   Volt-ohm-ammeter.

volt (V)   The basic practical unit of difference of potential, that is, of electrical pressure. 1 volt is the difference of potential produced across a resistance of 1 ohm by a current of 1 ampere.

voltage   Symbols, E, e, V. Electromotive force, or difference of potential; $E = IR$, where I is current and R is resistance. (Also see *volt*.)

voltage drop (VD)   In DC circuits, the voltage (E) set up across a resistance (R) carrying a current (I); $E = IR$. For alternating current, reactance (X) and impedance (Z) may be substituted for resistance where applicable.

volt-ammeter   A combination meter for measuring volts and amperes.

volt-ampere   Symbol, VA. Unit, watt. The simple product of voltage and current in volts and amperes, which gives the true power in a DC circuit and the apparent power in an AC circuit.

volt-milliammeter   A combination meter for measuring volts and milliamperes.

volt-ohm-ammeter   A multimeter for measuring volts, ohms, and amperes.

volt-ohmmeter   A combination meter for measuring volts and ohms.

volt-ohm-milliammeter (VOM)   A multimeter for measuring volts, ohms, and milliamperes. Such an instrument usually measures megohms and microamperes, too.

VOM   Volt-ohm-milliammeter.

W   1. Watt. 2. West. 3. Width.

wall box   A wall-mounted (usually metal) box enclosing circuit breakers, fuses, switches, or other devices.

wall outlet   A wall plug or socket usually mounted in a protective box or can, from the front of which it can be accessed, and recessed in a wall.

water analogy   The useful, but not wholly accurate, teaching device of comparing an electric current with the flow of water. In such a comparison, voltage is shown equivalent to water pressure, and current to the quantity (for example, gallons) of water flowing.

watt (W)   The practical unit of electric and other power. One watt is dissipated by a resistance of 1 ohm through which a current of 1 ampere flows.

Western Union joint   A strong splice of two wires made by tightly twisting a short portion of the tip of each wire along the body of the other. For increased ruggedness, the joint is often soldered. Also called Western Union splice.

wet cell   A battery cell having a liquid electrolyte. (Compare *dry cell.*)

winding   A coil of an inductor or transformer (for example, primary winding, secondary winding, output winding). Also, the coil of a motor or generator.

winding length   The length of a coil from the first turn to the last in a single-layer coil, or from the first turn to the last in one layer of a multilayer coil when all layers are identical (see Figure A–14).

wire   1. A metal strand or thread serving as a conductor of electricity. 2. To connect wires between points in a circuit.

wire duct   A conduit through which wires are run. Such ducts have several shapes, but generally are rectangular.

wire gauge   1. A system for specifying the characteristics of wire. (See

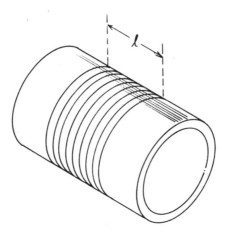

Figure A–14.   Winding length.

American Wire Gauge.) 2. A wire number governed by diameter (for example, 18-gauge wire or No. 18 wire). 3. A tool or instrument for measuring wire diameter or for determining wire number.

wireless   An early name for radio; it is still used in some countries. Sometimes for specificity radio is referred to as wireless telegraphy or wireless telephony.

wire splice   A strong, low resistance joint between (usually two) wires. (See, for example, *Western Union joint.*)

wire stripper   A hand tool or power machine for cutting the insulating jacket on a wire and removing it without cutting or nicking the wire.

wireways   Hinged-cover metal troughs for containing and protecting wires and cables. (Also see *wire duct.*)

wire-wrap connection   An electrical connection made by tightly wrapping a bare wire around a special terminal.

wiring diagram   See *circuit diagram.*

working voltage   The (usually maximum) voltage at which a circuit or device may be operated continuously with safety and reliability.

x   Shorthand representation of *trans* (for example, xfmr for transformer).

zinc-carbon cell   A primary cell in which the negative electrode is zinc, and the positive electrode is carbon. This type may be either wet or dry. (Also see *cell, dry cell,* and *primary cell.*

zip cord   A simple two-conductor, flexible power cord.

Index